Hezekiah Butterworth

Zigzag Journeys in Europe

Vacation Rambles in Historic Lands

Hezekiah Butterworth

Zigzag Journeys in Europe
Vacation Rambles in Historic Lands

ISBN/EAN: 9783744757690

Printed in Europe, USA, Canada, Australia, Japan

Cover: Foto ©Andreas Hilbeck / pixelio.de

More available books at **www.hansebooks.com**

IN EUROPE.

VACATION RAMBLES IN HISTORIC LANDS.

BY

HEZEKIAH BUTTERWORTH.

PREFACE.

THE aim of the publishers and writer, in preparing this volume for young people, is to give a view of the principal places in England and France where the most interesting events have occurred; and, by a free use of pictures and illustrative stories, to present historic views of the two countries in an entertaining and attractive manner.

An American teacher takes a class of boys on a vacation tour to England and France, and interests them in those places that illustrate the different periods of English and French history. It is his purpose to give them in this manner a picturesque view of present scenes and past events, and to leave on their minds an outline of history for careful reading to fill.

A few of the stories are legendary, as the "Jolly Harper Man" and the "Wise Men of Gotham;" but these illustrate the quaint manners and customs of the Middle Ages. Nearly all of the stories that relate to history are strictly true.

The illustrations of history, both by pencil and pen, are given in the disconnected way that a traveller would find them in his journeys;

PREFACE.

...they may be easily combined by memory in their chronological order, and made to form a harmonious series of pictures.

The writer has sought to amuse as well as to instruct, and for this purpose the personal experiences of the young travellers are in part given. Two of the boys, who have small means, make the trip in the cheapest possible manner. Tommy Toby meets the mishaps a thoughtless boy might experience. The other travellers have an eye for the literary and poetic scenes and incidents of the tour.

That the volume may amuse and entertain the young reader, and awaken in him a greater love of books of history, biography, and travel, is the hope of the publishers and the author.

WORCESTER ST., BOSTON, MASS.

CONTENTS.

Chapter		Page
I.	The Journey Proposed	3
II.	Tom Toby's Secret Society	12
III.	First Meeting of the Club	22
IV.	On the Atlantic	51
V.	The Land of Scott and Burns	71
VI.	Story Telling in Edinburgh	84
VII.	A Rainy Evening Story at Carlisle	104
VIII.	A Cloudless Day	119
IX.	A Series of Memorable Visits	135
X.	A Visit to Oxford and Woodstock	153
XI.	Letters and Excursions	160
XII.	London	173
XIII.	Belgium	205
XIV.	Upper Normandy	226
XV.	Paris	249
XVI.	Brittany	283
XVII.	Homeward	304

THE ZIGZAG SERIES.

BY

HEZEKIAH BUTTERWORTH.

ZIGZAG JOURNEYS IN EUROPE.
ZIGZAG JOURNEYS IN CLASSIC LANDS.
ZIGZAG JOURNEYS IN THE ORIENT.
ZIGZAG JOURNEYS IN THE OCCIDENT.
ZIGZAG JOURNEYS IN NORTHERN LANDS.
ZIGZAG JOURNEYS IN ACADIA.
ZIGZAG JOURNEYS IN THE LEVANT.
ZIGZAG JOURNEYS IN THE SUNNY SOUTH.
ZIGZAG JOURNEYS IN INDIA.
ZIGZAG JOURNEYS IN THE ANTIPODES.
ZIGZAG JOURNEYS IN THE BRITISH ISLES.
ZIGZAG JOURNEYS IN THE GREAT NORTH-WEST.

ESTES AND LAURIAT, Publishers,
BOSTON, MASS.

ILLUSTRATIONS.

	PAGE
"The Boy-king" . . . . . *Frontispiece.*	
Statue of William the Conqueror at Falise . . . . *Half-title.*	
It is Vacation	3
Tommy and the Bear	9
Tommy's Adventure	10
Norman Fisher-Girl	13
King Charles's Hiding-place	14
White Horse Hill	15
Street Scene in Normandy	16
Colonnade of the Louvre	17
Harold's Oath	23
Finding the Body of Harold	26
The Death of the Red King	27
St. Stephen's Church at Caen	30
Robert Throwing Himself on his Knees before his Prostrate Father	31
William the Conqueror Reviewing his Army	35
Mont St. Michel	37
Amazement of Christopher Sly . . .	46
Norman Peasant Girls	49
Pilot-Boat	53
Two of our Fellow-Travellers	55
A Steerage Passenger	56
Joan of Arc	59
Joan of Arc Recognizing the King . .	63
Joan of Arc Wounded	67
Signals	70
The Boys Consult the Barometer . .	72
Birthplace of Robert Burns	73
Edinburgh Castle	77

	PAGE
Holyrood Palace	79
Mary Stuart	80
Murder of Rizzio	81
Francis II. of France	86
Francis II. and Mary Stuart Love-making	89
At the Death-bed of Francis II. . . .	93
Mary Stuart Swearing she had never sought the Life of Elizabeth . . .	97
Cæsar's Legions Landing in Britain . .	104
Romans Invading Britain	105
Massacre of the Druids	106
Druid Sacrifice	107
The Hermit	111
Shamble Oak	121
Greendale Oak	122
Parliament Oak	123
Mortimer's Hole	124
Murder of Thomas à Becket	125
Richard's Farewell to the Holy Land .	129
Limestone Dwellings	133
Peveril of the Peak	137
The Boy at the Wheel	138
Boscobel	139
The Tomb of Richard Penderell . . .	139
King Charles's Hiding-place	140
Shakspeare	141
Anne Hathaway's Cottage	144
Ruins of Kenilworth Castle	145
Portrait of Elizabeth	149
Alfred and his Mother	153
Canute and his Courtiers	154

	PAGE		PAGE
Flight of Empress Maud	155	Tower of Joan of Arc, Rouen	229
Death of Latimer and Ridley	156	The Maid of Orleans	230
Rosamond's Bower	157	"It is Rather Hard Bread."	233
A Studious Monk	157	Death of St. Louis	235
An Old Time Student	158	Interior of St. Ouen	236
House of a Migrating Citizen	162	Palais de Justice, Rouen	237
Fac-simile of the Bayeux Tapestry	163	Northmen on an Expedition	238
St. Augustine's Appeal to Ethelbert	169	The Barques of the **Northmen before**	
The Saxon Priest Striking the Images	171	Paris	239
Westminster Abbey	174	Catharine de Medici	241
Trial of Charles I	177	Coligny	243
Burial of Richard	180	Charles IX. and Catharine de Medici	247
The Tower of London	181	The Goddess of Reason carried through	
Wolsey Served by Nobles	185	the Streets of Paris	251
Old Hampton Court	187	Garden of the Tuileries	255
Wolsey's Palace	188	Fountain in the Champs Elysées	257
Death of Cardinal Wolsey	189	Place de la Concorde	258
Children of Charles I.	190	Entrance to the Louvre	259
Oliver Cromwell	191	Fountain, Place de la Concorde	261
Queen Henrietta Maria	193	Man of the Iron Mask	263
Street Amusements	195	Versailles	**267**
Street Amusements	196	Little Trianon	**268**
"Ave you got a Penny?"	197	The Dauphin with the **Royal Family in**	
Victoria at the Age of Eight	200	the Assembly	269
Anger of King John	203	Forest of Fontainebleau	273
A Dutch Windmill	206	In the Wood at Fontainebleau	274
Dog-Carts	207	"Je ne comprends pas."	277
Street Scenes in Brussels	208	At Prayers	278
Hotel de Ville, Brussels	209	Clock Tower at Vire	283
Charlemagne in Council	210	Revoking the Edict of Nantes	291
Charlemagne at the Head of his **Army**	211	Fénelon and the Duke of Burgundy	295
Hotel de Ville, Ghent	212	The Cathedral at Nantes	298
Van Artevelde at his Door	213	Louis XV.	299
Charles the Rash Discovered	217	Molière	306
Capture of King John and his Son	227	The Reading of "Paul and Virginia."	307

ZIGZAG JOURNEYS;

OR,

VACATIONS IN HISTORIC LANDS.

CHAPTER I.

THE JOURNEY PROPOSED.

"THE school — is — dismissed."

The words fell hesitatingly, and it seemed to us regretfully, from the tutor's lips.

The dismission was for the spring vacation. It was at the close of a mild March day; there was a peculiar warmth in the blue sky and cloudless sunset; the south winds lightly stirred the pines, and through the open window wandered into the school-room.

"Dismissed!"

Usually at this word, on the last day of the term, every boy leaped to his feet: there would be a brief bustle, then Master Lewis would be seen seated alone amid the silence of the school-room.

But to-day there was something in the tone of the master's voice that checked the usual unseemly haste. Every boy remained in his seat, as though waiting for Master Lewis to say something more.

The master saw it, and choked with feeling. It was a little thing, the seeming unwillingness to part; but it indicated to both teacher and school an increasing respect and affection.

Master Lewis had learned to love his pupils: his hesitating words told them that. Every boy in his school loved Master Lewis: their conduct in remaining in their seats told him that.

The master stepped from his desk, as was his custom when about to say any thing unusually social and confidential.

"Boys," he said, "I wish to tell you frankly, and you deserve to know it, that I have become so attached to you during the winter term that I am sorry to part from you, even for a week's vacation."

"I wish we might pass the vacation together," said Frank Gray, — meaning by "we" the teacher and the school.

"I once read of a French teacher," said Ernest Wynn, "who used to travel with his scholars in the neighboring countries, during vacations.

"Wouldn't it be just grand if we could travel with Master Lewis during our summer vacation!" said Tom Toby, who, although the dullest scholar in the school, always became unexpectedly bright over any plan that promised an easy time.

"We might visit some country in Europe," said Ernest. "We should then be learning geography and history, and so our education would go on."

"It would help us also in the study of modern languages," said Frank Gray.

Tom Toby's sudden brightness of face seemed to be eclipsed by these last remarks.

"I think we had better travel in places nearer home, then."

"Why?" asked Frank.

"I was seasick once: it was *arful*."

"The sickness is a short and healthy one," said Frank.

"You will find it a healthy one, if you ever are rolling on the Atlantic, with

'Twice a thousand miles behind you, and a thousand miles before.'

I wouldn't be sick in that way again for any thing. I tell you 'twas *orful!*"

Master Lewis laughed at Tom's pointed objection.

"As to learning the languages," continued Tom, "I've noticed all the Frenchmen and Germans I have tried to talk with speak their own language very poorly."

Tom's percentages in the modern languages were the lowest of his class, and Master Lewis could not restrain a smile.

"I once tried to make a Frenchman understand that I thought Napoleon Bonaparte was the greatest man that ever lived. He kept saying, *Cela va sans dire, cela va sans dire!* [That is a matter of course.] I never knew what he meant to say: all I could make of it was, *That goes without saying any thing.*"

"The French teacher of whom I spoke," said Ernest Wynn, "used to allow his pupils to travel much on foot, and to visit such places as their love of history, geography, and natural science, made them most wish to see. So they journeyed in a zigzag way, and published a book called '*Voyages en zigzag.*'"

"I would not object to learning history, geography, and natural science in that way," said Tom Toby. "I should rather walk after history than study it the way I do now. I should prefer *riding* after it to walking, however. I wouldn't be cheated out of having a real good time during my summer vacation for any thing."

A shadow fell on Master Lewis's face, as though his feelings were hurt by something implied in Tom's remarks. Tom saw it.

"But — but I should have a real good time if I were with you, Master Lewis, even if it were on the Atlantic, or studying French in France."

"I have often thought I would like to travel with **my** boys abroad. I could take my first class, **if I could** secure their **parents**' consent, the coming summer."

"Good!"

Every boy joined in the exclamation. Tom's voice, however, was a little behind the others, — "-o-d."

"Let me suggest to **the class**," said Master **Lewis**, "that each member speak to his parents about this matter during the present vacation; and let each boy who can go send me in a letter during the week a map of the country **and** the places he would **most** like to visit. He can draw it in ink **or** pencil, and he need only **put** down upon it the places he would most like to see."

"Good!"

The exclamation was unanimous.

The boys left their seats.

Tom Toby's face had **become very** animated again. Presently the boys of the class were all gathered about him.

"I have a plan," said Tom. "It is just grand. **Let** us form a secret society, and call ourselves the Zigzagers!"

"Good!" unanimously.

"But why a secret society?" asked Frank Gray.

"There is something so mysterious about a secret society," said Tom. "Gives one such a good opinion of himself. Have a constitution, and by-laws, and wear a pin!"

The first class in Master Lewis's school parted in **high** spirits, their faces bright with smiles as they went out into the **light** of the March sunset.

Tom's last words on parting were: "Try to think up a secret for the society it should be something surprising."

The first class in Master Lewis's school numbered **six** boys: —

FRANK GRAY,	THOMAS TOBY,
ERNEST WYNN,	GEORGE HOWE, **and**
WYLLYS WYNN,	LEANDER TOWLE.

Frank Gray was the oldest boy and finest scholar in the school. He was about fifteen years of age; was tall and manly, and was more intimate with Master Lewis than with any of his schoolmates. Thomas Toby, who disliked Frank's precise manners and rather unsocial ways, used to call him "Lord I." Frank, however, was not intentionally reserved: he was merely studious in his leisure, and best liked the society of those from whom he could learn the most.

Ernest and Wyllys Wynn were brothers. Ernest had made himself popular at school by his generous, affectionate disposition, and his ready sympathy for any one in distress. He lived, as it were, a life outside of himself; and his interest in the best good of others made for himself unconsciously a pure and lovable character. He was fond of music, and an agreeable singer: he liked the old English and Scottish ballads, and so sung the songs of true feeling that every one is eager to hear.

He often went to an almshouse near Master Lewis's to sing to the old people there. The paupers all loved him, and clustered eagerly around him when he appeared. His songs recalled their childhood scenes in other lands. On fine summer evenings he might often be seen on the lawn before the charitable institution, with a crowd of poor people around him, whom he delighted with "Robin Ruff and Gaffer Green," "The Mistletoe Bough," "Highland Mary," "The Vale of Avoca," "Robin Adair," or something aptly selected to awaken tender feelings and associations.

Nearly all the children of the town seemed to know him, and regard him as a friend, and used often to run out to meet him when he appeared in the street. Master Lewis, in speaking of Ernest, once quoted Madame de Sévigné's remark, "The true mark of a good heart is its capacity for loving." It was meant to be a picture, and it was a true one.

Wyllys Wynn was much like his brother, and a very close friendship existed between them. He was fond of history and poetry; he wrote finely, and usually took the first prize for composition.

Tom Toby was quite a different character. He was just a *boy*, in the common sense of the word. In whatever he attempted to do, he was sure to blunder, and was as sure to turn the blunder to some comical account. He had a way of making fun of himself, and of inciting others to laugh at his own expense, which Master Lewis was disposed to censure as wanting in proper self-respect.

Tom had no particular friend. He seemed to like all boys alike, except those whom he thought insincere and affected, and such were the butt of his sharp wit and ready ridicule.

Tom was famous among the boys for telling stories, and these often related to his own mishaps. A knot of boys was often seen gathered around him to listen to his random talk, his wit, and his day dreams. Though a poor scholar, he was an apt talker, and almost any subject would furnish him a text.

His father was a Maine lumber-dealer, and he had spent much time with his father in the logging camps and backwoods towns of the Pine Tree State. His adventures in these regions, told in his droll way, often excited the wonder of his companions.

"Did you ever see a bear in the backwoods?" one of the boys asked him one day.

"I never saw a live one but once."

"What did you do?"

"Do? I received a polite bow from him, and then I remembered that I was wanted at home, and went home immediately.

"It was this way"—All of the boys of the class now gathered around Tommy, as was the custom when he seemed about to tell one of his odd stories.

"I attempted one day to rob a pigeon-woodpecker's nest which I had found in one of the old logging roads that had not been used for several years. The nest was in a big hollow tree. The top of the tree had blown off, leaving a trunk some twelve or fifteen feet high.

THE JOURNEY PROPOSED.

"These woodpeckers make a hole for their nest so large that you can run the whole length of your arm into it. I had long wanted a few eggs from one of these birds' nests. I had heard the lumber-men tell how white and handsome the eggs are.

"I was climbing up the tree very fast, my heart beating like a trip-hammer, when I heard a scratching sound inside the big trunk, and then a shaking at the top. I thought it very mysterious. I stopped, and looked up. I saw something black, like a fur cap. I opened my eyes and mouth so as to take a big look, and just then *out popped a bear's head* from the top of the trunk, and looked over very inquiringly. I just looked once. He seemed to recognize me. He bowed. Then I remembered that father had said I must come home early. I dropped to the ground, and I never picked up my feet so lively before in my life. I *flew*. When I got safely out of the woods, I thought of the woodpecker. I never felt so glad for any bird in my life. What a narrow escape that bird had! *I had been there myself,* and knew. I wouldn't have robbed her nest for any thing after that.

"'No, not I.'"

When Tommy first came to the boarding-school, he greatly amused his companions one day by attempting to ride on the hose of a street-sprinkler's cart, when it was not in action. He had never seen such a carriage, and thought it offered a wonderfully convenient arrangement for riding behind. Presently the driver raised the lever, and the amazed lad found himself caught in the shower, and tumbled into the dirt.

"Why didn't you tell me the thing was bewitched?" said he, as the boys gathered around him.

But his indignation immediately subsided, and rubbing off the water and dirt, and discovering the use of the cart, he was soon found laughing as heartily as the others, and quite outdid them in relating to Master Lewis the odd adventure.

George Howe and Leander Towle were cousins and very intimate friends. They were unlike Frank Gray and the Wynns. They cared little for poetry, art, or music. They stood well in their classes in mathematics and the exact sciences, were fond of boating and out-of-door sports, and both were warm friends of Tom Toby.

The pleasant relations that existed between the teacher and the school also prevailed to a great degree among the lads themselves. Frank Gray and Tommy Toby, being quite unlike, sometimes had a tilt in words; but, as Frank was a gentleman by nature and training, and as Tommy had tender feelings, their differences were easily harmonized. The mild manners and good sense of Master Lewis seemed to impress themselves strongly on the characters of his pupils. Tommy Toby, who was often thoughtless in his conduct, was almost the only exception to the rule.

CHAPTER II.

TOM TOBY'S SECRET SOCIETY.

PLANS FOR THE JOURNEY. — THE BOYS' LETTERS TO MASTER LEWIS. — TOM TOBY'S PLANS. — THE NEW SOCIETY. — MASTER LEWIS ARRANGES A CHEAP TOUR FOR GEORGE AND LEANDER. — WHAT MAY BE SEEN FOR $100.

FROM Frank Gray, Master Lewis received the following letter early in vacation-week: —

CAMBRIDGE, MASS., March 20.

MY DEAR FRIEND AND TEACHER:

My good father has consented for me to go.

He thinks that the tour, to be a really profitable one, should be short, and that it would be better to attempt to visit only a portion of a single country.

I have decided what country I would most like to visit. It is "Ler Normandy," the scene of the most romantic events of both English and French history.

I would go from Boston to London; from London to Dieppe; and then I would make partly on foot a zigzag journey to the places indicated on the enclosed map of Normandy, and such others, including Paris, as you may suggest.

The old towns on the coast of Normandy are especially beautiful in summer, with their cool harbors, fine landscapes, and historic ruins. I am told that they are favorite places of resort of both the English and French people, and that they give one delightful insights of the best social life.

In this journey, we would have views of London and Paris, and would be able to study that part of France whose history is associated with old English wars, and that is most famous in romance and song.

I make the suggestion at your own request. You are the better judge in the whole matter, and it will give my father pleasure to adopt any plan for me you may think advisable.

I thank you again for the invitation, and father wishes me to express to you his sense of your kindness.

I wish you a most pleasant vacation, and am

    Affectionately yours,

            FRANK GRAY.

"Fan me with a feather!" Tom Toby used sometimes to say after reading one of Frank's letters; and we are not sure but this careful note would have tempted a light remark, had he ever seen it.

Soon after Frank's note, came a note from the Wynns: —

NORMAN FISHER-GIRL.

CONCORD, MASS., March 22.

DEAR TEACHER:

Father thinks so favorably of your kind invitation that we venture to express our preference for a route of travel.

It is a very simple one. We would go from Boston to Liverpool, and walk from Liverpool, to London, *en zigzag*.

This would take us through the heart of England, and enable us to visit such historic places as Boscobel, where Charles II. was concealed after the battle of Worcester, old Nottingham, Kenilworth, Oxford, and Godstowe Nunnery, Stratford-on-Avon, White Horse Hill, and a great number of old English villages and ruins.

Or we would go to Glasgow, thence to Edinburgh, and then make short journeys towards London, visiting Abbotsford, Melrose, and the ruins on the Border.

KING CHARLES'S HIDING-PLACE.

We are reading Walter Scott's "Kenilworth." The book, as you may have guessed, has caused us to set our affections strongly on the middle of England as the scene of our proposed tour.

With kind remembrances of all your kindness to us.

ERNEST WYNN.
WYLLYS WYNN.

Later came a characteristic note from two of the other boys.

DEAR TEACHER, — Our parents are desirous for us to go, but can hardly afford the expense. We have permission to accept your invitation, if we will travel so cheaply that the cost to each will not be more than $100. Can this be done? We are willing to go and return in the steerage, travel third-class, and take shilling lodgings, and eat plain food. We would prefer a tour through the great manufacturing towns of Scotland and England.

Respectfully,

GEORGE HOWE.
LEANDER TOWLE.

WHITE HORSE HILL.

Mother has been crying. She is afraid, if I go to Europe, I will never come back again.

Father thinks that there is no danger of that.

If I must go across the sea, I would prefer to go — anywhere *you* like, only take the shortest route and fastest steamer over the water.

Were you ever sick on the ocean?

I am going to organize a society of travellers in the school, — a secret society that will pledge each other never-ending friendship and assistance.

I may need assistance myself in my life. Father thinks I shall.

I am trying to think of a secret for the society. I can think of hardly any thing that the rest of the world do not know.

Hope you are well.

TOMMY.

HOTEL INN IN NORMANDY.

The spring and summer term — the session lasted through April, May, and June — opened under unusually promising circumstances. The prospect of the journey of the first class seemed to stimulate the whole school: in fact, little else was talked of out of school-hours.

Master Lewis's customary address at the close of the first day of the term was waited with impatient interest. When the time came for it, there was almost a painful silence in the school-room.

"I shall speak first," said Master Lewis, "on the subject about which your conduct tells me you are most eager to hear. I have decided to take the journey abroad with the first class *this* year" —

There was suppressed applause by the class.

"Next year I hope to visit Switzerland and Italy, with all the members of the school who can go, if this proposed journey should prove a success. I say this, so that the second and third classes may feel that they, too, have an interest in this general plan."

There was a burst of applause by the whole school.

"I thank the boys of the first class for their letters and suggestions about the route to be decided upon. I think I have a plan that will be acceptable to you all. We will go first to Glasgow, will journey *en zigzag* to London; will there take the steamer for Antwerp, and will

COLONNADE OF THE LOUVRE.

make a zigzag tour from Ghent to St. Malo, taking a glance at Belgium. a view of the whole of Normandy and the picturesque part of Brittany. including a visit to Paris and a view of its beautiful palaces and parks.

"As a preparation for this tour, I shall require the class to give special attention to the French language and to English and French history during the term."

Every thing that Master Lewis said or did was popular with the boys, but no decision ever received more emphatic applause.

Tom Toby was busy at once, forming his secret society. He called a meeting of the boys on the evening of the very first school-day, in his room. The Wynns entered willingly into his plan, and George Howe and Leander Towle warmly supported it. Frank Gray, however, treated the matter rather indifferently, a circumstance that Tommy quickly observed.

"The first question to be decided," said Tommy, when the boys had met in his room, "is, Shall we organize a secret society?"

The Wynns asked Frank Gray his opinion.

"I should prefer to hold my opinion in reserve, until I understand what the object of the society is to be."

"It is to have a grip just like *that*," said Tommy, seizing Frank by the hand, "one that takes the conceit all out of you, and makes you remember who are your friends for ever."

"Then I do not think I shall care to join," said Frank, rubbing his crushed hand on his knee. "I shall probably remember you as long as I shall care to, without making any such arrangement."

"I think a school society is a good thing," said Ernest Wynn, mildly. "It promotes lasting friendships."—

"Good for you!" said Tommy. "That's just what I wanted to say. 'It promotes lasting friendship,' and, like a salve, it takes the conceit"—

"It stimulates one to do his best, and"—

"That's it exactly," said Tommy. "I hope you all hear."

"Let's quit joking," said George Howe, in a matter-of-fact way. "A society for the purpose of reading and studying about the places we are to visit and for correspondence with each other, when a part of us are abroad, would be an excellent thing. I hope we may have such a society, and shall make our very best boy President of it."

"Who may that be?" said Frank.

"I," said Tommy, teasingly. "I thought you knew."

"I believe it is decided to call the society the Zigzag Travellers," said George.

"A promising name," said Frank, who was decidedly out of humor. "I would suggest the Zigzag Club."

"I would nominate for President Wyllys Wynn."

"I agree to the nomination," said Frank.

"And so do I," said Tommy Toby: "at last, Frank and I are agreed."

"Who will prepare the rules for the society?" asked Frank.

"George Howe," said Ernest.

To this all the boys agreed.

"Who shall decide upon a secret?" asked Wyllys.

"I would nominate Tommy Toby," said Frank.

Tom was unanimously elected.

The next evening a second meeting of the society was held, to which all the boys in the school were invited. It was decided to call the society "The Zigzag Club." Charles Wyman, one of the second-class boys, was appointed its Secretary, and general rules were adopted for the conduct of its meetings. All of the boys, sixteen in number, became members.

It was decided that the first formal meeting of the club for literary exercises should be held in a fortnight, and that on that occasion each boy of the first class should relate some historic story associated with one of the places he expected to visit, and it was suggested that the stories of the first meeting be confined to *Normandy*. Wyllys Wynn was asked to sing some French or Norman song on the occasion, and the Secretary was instructed to invite Master Lewis to be present, and to deliver an address.

Tommy Toby had been very reserved since the first meeting of the club. He had been quite ignored, and his feelings were hurt.

"Are you sure you treated Tommy quite right at the first meeting?" asked Ernest Wynn of Frank Gray, quietly, as he observed Tom's injured look at the second meeting of the club.

"I fear I was not quite gentlemanly," said Frank. "But I had no wish to join a society gotten up merely for fun."

"Tommy's suggestion was the beginning of the club," said Ernest. "Let's give him a vote of thanks."

"I will offer the resolution," said Frank.

"Let us close this meeting," said Frank, "by recognizing the debt we owe to one of our members. Thomas Toby is the real founder of this club. I did not feel much interested in it at first. I do now. Let us give Thomas a vote of thanks."

Every boy applauded the motion, which was passed enthusiastically.

Tommy's face brightened, and his eyes filled with tears.

"O Frank," he said, "how could you? Ernest Wynn was at the bottom of this, wasn't he?"

"Yes," said Frank.

"Well, Ernest *is* a better fellow than I."

"Or I."

"We both are all right now!"

"Yes."

"Have you decided upon a secret?" continued Frank.

"I have thought much about it," answered Tom.

"And what is the result?"

"I wish you to go," he said; "and I think a most profitable tour can be made in the way you propose for $100. You can at least visit Glasgow, Edinburgh, Birmingham, London, and Paris, and spend three days each in the three great capital cities. The information you would thus gain would be of great value to you. I thus estimate the probable expense to each: —

Steerage passage to go and return	$50.00
Glasgow to Edinburgh, 2s. 6d., or	.60
Edinburgh to London, and London to Paris by way of Dieppe, about £3, or	14.40
Shilling lodgings and meals for fourteen days	14.00
Miscellaneous expenses	11.00
	$90.00

"I will do my best to make your expenses as light as possible. I am told that one can live comfortably on four shillings a day in Scotland and England, and for five francs a day in Paris. You will not be able to enjoy our walks in historic places outside of the great cities, and you will probably be obliged to return before the rest of the party; but the very restraint you will have to use will be a good experience for you. As Franklin once said, 'A good kick out of doors is worth all the rich uncles in the world.' It is good for one to bear the yoke in his youth. You see what I mean, — self-reliance, independence! I am not altogether sorry that you will be compelled to make the journey in this way."

The boys thanked their teacher.

When they had left him, George Howe said decidedly, —

"I never respected any teacher as much as I do Master Lewis. How nobly he has treated us!"

CHAPTER III.

FIRST MEETING OF THE CLUB.

NORMANDY. — STORY OF THE NEW FOREST AND THE RED KING. — STORY OF ROBERT OF NORMANDY. — STORY OF THE WHITE SHIP. STORY OF THE FROLICSOME DUKE AND THE TINKER'S GOOD FORTUNE. — MASTER LEWIS COMMENDS THE CLUB. — THE SECRET.

HEN the boys were allowed to go to Boston, — once a week, — they had access to the fine Public Library of which that city is justly so proud. It was observed that the whole character of their reading changed from merely entertaining to the most instructive books, after the forming of the Club. Such picturesque historical works as Guizot's "France" and "England," Palgrave's "Norman Conquest," Froude's "England," Agnes Strickland's "Lives of the Queens," became especial favorites. Even Tommy Toby read through Dickens's Child's History of England, several of Abbott's short histories of the kings and queens, and a book of marvellous old English ballads.

HAROLD'S OATH.

The Club met as appointed. Each of the six boys had made his best preparation for the exercises of the evening. All the boys were present; and Master Lewis and his little daughter Florence sat beside young President Wynn, on the platform.

Wyllys Wynn was the first speaker.

"Although President of the Club," he said, "I am expected to take part in these exercises, and have been asked to present my story first. Normandy is our subject to-night, and there is no name that is so famously associated with the old Norman cities we expect to visit — Caen, Falaise, Rouen, Fécamp, St. Valery — as that of William the Conqueror. I will tell you the story of his life, and call it

THE NEW FOREST.

"About eight hundred years ago, William, Duke of Normandy, aspired to become King of England, and to wear the crown whose rightful claimant was Edgar Atheling. He made Harold, another heir to the English crown, support his claim, and take an oath to be true to him. To make Harold feel how solemn was an oath, he obliged him to swear it over a chest full of dead men's bones.

"But Harold disregarded the oath that he had taken over the chest of bones in Normandy; and, when old Edward, who was called The Confessor, died, he seized the crown and royal treasure for himself, being counselled to do so by an assembly of nobles called the Witenagemote.

"Duke William was an ambitious and a fiery-minded man. He gathered an army of sixty thousand men, and a fleet of a thousand vessels and transports; and one September day he sailed from St. Valery with his army and fleet, the trumpets sounding and a thousand banners rising to the wind. His own ship had many-colored sails: from its mast floated the banner of the three Norman Lions; and a golden boy, pointing to England, glittered on the prow.

"This fleet came into the harbor of Pevensey. He led his army to Hastings, and there, on a bright afternoon in October, he met the army of Harold.

"Duke William reviewed his army, and caused his men to pray for victory ere they laid down beneath the moon and stars to rest. In the morning, they sung an ode, called the War Song of Roland; then a battle was fought, and the three Norman Lions at night waved triumphantly over the field.

FINDING THE BODY OF HAROLD.

"Harold was slain, and the monks wandered over the battle-ground to find his body. It was discovered at last, a despoiled and discrowned figure, by Edith Swansneck, a beautiful girl who loved Harold and whom the dead king had loved.

"Then William returned to Normandy. Fécamp blazed in his honor, and all the cities received him with loud acclaim.

"A hard king was Duke William. With his great army of Normans, he marched over England, suppressing all who opposed him. The rivers were tinged with blood, the beautiful English towns were reduced to ash-heaps, the land was blackened with fire — he is said to have killed or maimed a hundred thousand people.

"Having conquered England, he sought enjoyment, and turned his

THE DEATH OF THE RED KING.

attention to field-sports and to hunting. He had sixty-eight royal forests, full of stags and deer; but he permitted no one but himself and the people of his court to hunt in them.

"At Winchester, he thought it would be a fine thing to have a great hunting-park near his residence. There was a tract of country in the county of Hampshire, very picturesque and beautiful, that he determined to use for this purpose. But there were churches scattered among the hills; and thousands of peasants dwelt here, who had rude but happy homes.

"William cared little for the churches and less for the homes of the peasants; so he sent soldiers to burn the former, and to drive the people away from the latter.

"Nothing was done by the ruthless king to supply the wants of the people, or to relieve their misery. They left their native hills with wailing and weeping and wringing of hands, uttering imprecations on the head of the Conqueror and upon his race.

"The stags multiplied, and the deer increased; and delightful to the Norman was the New Forest, on the golden autumn days.

"One day, one of the king's sons, a fair-haired youth, named Richard, went to hunt in this New Forest.

"He encountered a stag. The animal, maddened by the attack, rushed upon the prince, and killed him.

"As the dead body was borne from the forest, broken and stained with blood, the people said that this was a beginning of the reckoning God would make with William, and that the New Forest would prove an unquiet place to the Conqueror and to those of his blood.

"Foolish and superstitious stories began to be circulated. The people said that the New Forest was haunted; that spirits were seen, by moonlight, gliding among the dusky trees; that demons revelled there when the tempest arose, and the lightnings flashed, and the rain dashed on the great oaks. The old foresters did not wish to return to it now. They talked of it in low whispers, as of a place accursed.

"At last William died. It was a bitter death. The Conqueror trembled before that Conqueror to whom the princes of the earth must yield.

"It is said that, when he had reached the height of his fame, he declared that he would surrender his crowns and kingdom to know again 'peace of mind, the love of a true friend, or the innocent sleep of a child.'

"When his last hour drew near, the nobles fled from his bedside. His servants pillaged the apartment where he died, and rolled the dead body from the bed, and left it lying on the floor. A good knight took it up, and carried it to St. Stephen's Church, at Caen.

ST. STEPHEN'S CHURCH AT CAEN.

ROBERT THROWING HIMSELF ON HIS KNEES BEFORE HIS PROSTRATE FATHER

"He left three sons, William Rufus, Robert, and Henry. To the first he bequeathed England, to the second Normandy, and to the last £5,000.

"William Rufus now became king of England. He was called the Red King, because he had a red face and red hair; and a red king he proved to be, in another sense.

"The Red King, like his father, quarrelled with everybody, and, like him, sought and found enjoyment by hunting in the New Forest.

"One pleasant day in May, when the leaves were tender, and the ferny hills were sunny and sprinkled with flowers, another Richard, the son of Robert of Normandy, went to hunt in the New Forest. After a merry time, he was accidentally shot by an arrow. Again a mournful retinue came out of the forest, bearing the body of a prince, stained with blood.

"August came, with its young deer and newly fledged birds. The Red King, with his brother Henry and a great court-party, went to the New Forest, to spend some days in hunting and feasting. The first day sped merrily, and was followed by a banquet. It was held at a place called Malwood-Keep, a famous lodge for royal hunting-parties.

"The next night, a man with a coal-cart was riding in the New Forest, when he discovered a body lying by the way, pierced by an arrow in the breast. He laid it in his dirty cart, and jogged on. It was the Red King.

"Many stories are told of the manner in which the king was killed. Some say that he was accidentally shot by Sir Walter Tyrrel, a famous hunter in those days.

"It is said that the king and Sir Walter came upon a stag. The king drew his bow, and the string broke.

"'Shoot, Walter!' said the king.

"The arrow flew, struck a tree, glanced, and buried itself in the king's breast. He died where the poor peasants had foretold he would die, in the New Forest.

Frank Gray followed: —

"Our President has told you the history of William the Conqueror and of one of his sons, in his story of the New Forest. I will try to tell you

THE STORY OF ROBERT OF NORMANDY.

"Robert of Normandy was the second son of the Conqueror, and succeeded his father in the dukedom. He was unlike the rest of the Conqueror's sons, — an easy, generous, pleasure-loving fellow; honest in heart, and believing with wonderful simplicity that the world was all sunshine, and that all the people in it were much like himself.

"I am sorry to say, however, that he once rebelled against his father, whom he asked to give him the old Norman kingdom. 'I am not apt to undress before I go to bed,' said the Conqueror.

"He began to rule independently, and William besieged him in the old fortress of Gerberoi.

"In the midst of the battle, Robert unseated a tall knight, and was about to despatch him, when he found him to be his father.

"He was greatly touched at the discovery, and kneeling down said 'I pray you forgive me.' He then raised his father, and they were reconciled.

"There is a castle in Normandy, which we hope to visit, — a mountain of towers rising out of the sea. Pagan priests possessed it, holy hermits succeeded them, and the Norman Dukes regarded it as their stronghold

WILLIAM THE CONQUEROR REVIEWING HIS ARMY.

I have brought with me a picture of it, that you may see. It is a fortress built upon a rock; and, when the great tide sweeps in, it stands in the sea, lofty and doubly guarded.

"The Red King and Robert once were engaged in a war with their brother Henry, who shut himself up in this fortress. At last, the water in the fortress failed. The Red King was happy, but Robert began to pity his famishing brother. So he sent him some bottles of wine.

"'A fine way to wage war,' said the Red King.

"'What,' said Robert, 'shall we let our brother die of thirst? Where shall we get another, when he is gone?'

We will see how Henry returned this love and brotherly kindness.

"It was considered very pious, in those rude times, for a person to make a pilgrimage to Jerusalem, in order to visit the Holy Sepulchre. The Turks, who held the Holy City, abused the Christian pilgrims. An eloquent and a fiery-minded monk, called Peter the Hermit, believing it to be the duty of the Christian princes to wrest the Holy Sepulchre from the power of the Turks, began to urge his opinions throughout Europe. An intense excitement was created.

"Among his most fervent disciples was **Robert of Normandy**. In his enthusiasm, the thoughtless, generous-hearted fellow sold his dominions for a certain period to the Red King, and with the money equipped a splendid retinue of knights and soldiers for service in the Holy Land.

"He went to Jerusalem at the head of this glittering train, and, in union with other Christian princes and nobles, besieged the Holy City, subdued its defenders, and obtained possession of the Saviour's tomb.

"Robert was one of the most conspicuous leaders in the first crusade; and, of all the princes who aided in the recovery of the Holy Sepulchre, he sacrificed the most.

"When he returned from the East, he stopped in Italy. He was fond of minstrelsy, and of works of art; and he feasted his eyes on the fading grandeur of the old Italian cities. As he was the rightful claimant to the throne of England, after the death of the Red King, and as his exploits in the Holy Land had added to his fame, the Italians

Italy, enamoured of Sibylla; and Henry, without waiting to see him buried, had seized the royal treasure and the diadem, telling the nobles that Robert had become King of Jerusalem.

"Having established his government, he was prepared to give Robert a hot reception, if he should make any trouble about the matter on his return.

"Robert, of course, asserted his claim to the throne. Some of the nobles sustained Henry in his usurpation, others were for Robert.

"Henry, however, by dint of much fawning and lying, persuaded Robert to relinquish his claim to England, and to be content with the little duchy of Normandy, and with a pension, which he promised to pay.

"So the good-natured Robert governed in Normandy, and a good-natured government he had. He was so weak and good-natured that he used to allow his servants to steal his clothes, while he was lying in bed in the morning.

"Henry, like the Red King before him, thought that Robert's government was rather loose, and that it would be a very benevolent thing to relieve the Normans of his misrule. For this reason, he went over to Normandy with an army, took possession of the country, and established his own hard rule, thus stealing from his brother the fair-kied duchy that the Conqueror had given him. Having accomplished this, he settled it that Robert was a very troublesome fellow, and that the proper place for him was a prison; and he accordingly put him in one.

"He was not satisfied even then.

"One day there appeared in the apartments of the castle where Robert was confined some stone-hearted men, by order from the king. They heated a piece of metal red-hot, and then deliberately burned out poor Robert's eyes.

"Beautiful, loving eyes they were; and what sights they had seen, — the minarets of the East glimmering in the hot sun and shady moon, the cool palm-groves along the Jordan, the splendid streets of Antioch, the City of the Great King, the Holy Sepulchre with its golden lamps, Italy with its deep skies and empurpled hills! Twenty-eight years was poor Robert imprisoned, and then he died."

Frank's contribution was well received.

"I would like to add something to the touching narrative we have just heard," said Master Lewis. "I would like to tell you about the great sorrow that came to King Henry, after he had so wronged his brother. Allow me to relate to you

THE STORY OF THE WHITE SHIP.

"Henry had a son — Prince Henry — whom he intensely loved. The prince was wild and dissipated, and as much a despot at heart as his father. He once boasted that, when he became king, he would yoke the English to the plough, like oxen.

"The king's plottings, and much of his cruel treatment of his brother Robert, sprang from his strong desire that this son might succeed him on the throne.

"Did Prince Henry succeed his father as king?

"The people of Normandy and other French territories under the Norman crown rebelled against Henry. The king, by the aid of the Pope, pacified the discontented people by fair promises, and a peace was made, upon which the king and the prince and a great retinue of nobles went to Normandy, to arrange some very important matters of state.

"During this state visit, the Norman nobles were induced to recognize, with great pomp, Prince Henry as the successor to the king and a marriage was contracted for the prince.

"In honor of these events, there were gala-days and festivals, and every scene of rejoicing the prince was the glittering star.

"The heart of the king swelled with pride. He had reason to hope that all his plottings. and pilferings of crowns and dominions, were about to end happily. The future seemed almost without a cloud.

"One bright day in autumn, after these events, the prince and a gay party prepared to embark for England.

"There came to the king a man by the name of Fitz-Stephen, who said that he was the son of the sea-captain who conveyed the Conqueror to England on the ship with many-colored sails. He said, also, that he had a beautiful ship, all white, and manned by fifty sea-browned sailors, and that he would deem it a great honor to take the royal party to England.

"'I have ordered my ship,' said the king. after a little deliberation; but yours shall have the honor of conveying the prince and young nobles to England.'

"So the prince, and one hundred and twenty-two nobles, and eighteen ladies of rank, all young, and full of merry life, went on board of the White Ship.

"The king sailed away while it was yet day, leaving the prince and his company still in the harbor.

"'Now,' said the prince. 'the king has gone, we will have a merry-making. The time is ours, and we can spend it right jovially on the deck of our beautiful ship.'

"He then ordered Fitz-Stephen to provide three casks of wine for the fifty sailors. The harbor grew dusky, and the hunter's moon rose, shimmering the wide waters. The wine flowed freely, the nobles danced, and the beautiful ladies joined heartily in the revelries.

"The great sea sobbed before and around them. but merry music filled their ears.

"At length, they shot out of the moonlit harbor. The sailors were excited and half-drunk. The royal party urged them to row with speed, in order to overtake the vessels of the king. Fitz-Stephen was in the same condition as his crew, and steered recklessly.

"Soon there came a terrific crash. The White Ship reeled and reeled, but went no farther. She had struck upon rocks, and the mirth was turned to wailing and woe.

"As the ship was sinking, the prince leaped on board a boat. As he was rowed away, he heard his sister calling for help from the deck of the staggering vessel. Putting back, he reached the place just as the White Ship was making her last plunge. Great numbers of the terrified and desperate young men leaped on board of the boat. It overturned, and the prince went down in the deep waters.

"Thus in a moment were baffled the purposes of King Henry for so many guilty years; and, of the three hundred souls that made merry in the moonlit harbor of Baltleur, but one survived to tell the dismal tale.

"For some days no one dared to approach the king with the dreadful intelligence. At length, a little boy was sent to him to break the news, who, weeping, knelt at his feet, and told him that the White Ship was lost, and the prince had perished. The king fell to the floor as dead. The historians tell us that he never smiled again.

"I do not greatly pity him; for he lied again, and he stole again and he made the people suffer again, and I have little doubt that he smiled again, when some plot of his crafty old age had ended to his liking.

"Mrs. Hemans, in a short historical poem, tenderly touches on the sorrow of King Henry for the lost prince; and, as I have not alluded to that sorrow in a very charitable spirit, I will quote the stanzas.—

HE NEVER SMILED AGAIN.

"The bark that held a prince went down,
　The sweeping waves roll'd on;
And what was England's glorious crown
　To him that wept a son?
He lived, — for life may long be borne
　Ere sorrow break its chain;
Why comes not death for those who mourn?—
　He never smiled again!

There stood proud forms around his throne.
  The stately and the brave ;
But which could fill the place of one,
  That one beneath the wave ?
Before him pass'd the young and fair,
  In pleasure's reckless train :
But seas dash'd o'er his son's bright hair —
  He never smiled again !

He sat where festal bowls went round,
  He heard the minstrel sing,
He saw the tourney's victor crown'd,
  Amidst the knightly ring :
A murmur of the restless deep
  Was blent with every strain,
A voice of winds that would not sleep —
  He never smiled again.

Hearts, in that time, closed o'er the trace
  Of vows once fondly pour'd,
And strangers took the kinsman's place
  At many a joyous board ;
Graves, which true love had bathed with tears,
  Were left to heaven's bright rain,
Fresh hopes were born for other years —
  He never smiled again ! "

TOMMY TOBY'S STORY OF THE FROLICSOME DUKE.

Tom Toby's turn came next, and at the announcement of his name there was a sudden lighting up of faces. Tom's face, which was usually rather comical, assumed a more mirth-loving expression than ever.

"You said," he began, "that we were to visit Ghent and Bruges. I believe these towns were in old Flanders, and that Flanders was in Burgundy. One of the most clever rulers of whom I ever read was Philip the Good, Duke of Burgundy, though he had some faults when he used to be young like me.

"The good Duke married Eleonora, sister to the King of Portugal. The wedding was celebrated in great pomp at Bruges, and the merry-makings lasted a week.

"Christopher Sly was a tinker, and a tinker was a man who used to 'roam the countries around,' crying, 'Old brass to mend!' and who repaired the good people's broken pots and kettles.

"Christopher heard of the great wedding in his travels, and came to Bruges to enjoy the merry-making with the rest.

"He had only one pair of breeches, and they were made of leather. He deemed them suitable for all occasions. He had never arrived at the luxury of a coat, but in its place he wore a large leather apron, which covered his great shoulders, like the armor of a knight.

"Christopher had one bad habit. He loved ale overmuch, and he used to drink so deeply on festive occasions as to affect the steadiness both of his mind and body.

"Christopher enjoyed the gala-days. He mingled in the gay processions that followed the ducal pair to the tournament; he gazed with loyal pride on the horses with their trappings of crimson and gold; he followed the falconers to the hunting-parks, and listened to the music that led the dance at night in the torch-lit palace.

"The ducal wedding took place in the deep of winter; and one night, soon after the joyful event, and while Bruges was yet given up to festivities, there fell a great snow-storm, blocking the streets and silencing the town.

"Christopher's money was gone, and the falling weather chilled not only his blood, but his spirits. He wandered about in the storm, going from ale-house to ale-house, and receiving hospitality, until the town of Bruges seemed to revolve around him as its inhabitants around the Duke. Still he plodded away through the streets, longing to see the warm fires glow and the torches gleam in the ducal palace. When he had nearly reached the palace, the town began to spin and whirl around him at such a rate that presently he sank in the chilly snow and knew no more.

"'I am tired of the palace,' said the Duke to some courtiers. 'Let us go into the streets this blustering night: it may be that we shall meet with an adventure.'

"The Duke, with a few muffled followers, glided out of one of the palace gates, and the gleamings of their lanterns shot down the street. Presently the Duke stumbled over some object, lying half-buried in the snow.

"'What's here?'

"'A dead man,' answered a courtier.

"'A drunken tinker,' answered an attendant, turning over the body of a man lying like a log in the snow. 'How he snores! Dead drunk, as I live!'

"'He would perish here before morning,' said the Duke.

"'What is to be done?' asked a courtier.

"'Take him to the palace, and we will have some sport with him. I will cause him to be washed and dressed and perfumed, and to be laid in a chamber of state. He will awake sober in the morning, when we will persuade him that *he* is the Duke, and that we are his attendants. To-morrow the whole Court of Burgundy shall serve a poor tinker!'

"The attendants carried the unconscious tinker to the palace, where they washed him, and, putting upon him an elegant night-dress, laid him on a silk-curtained bed, in a very gorgeous chamber.

"The poor tinker, on waking in the morning, looked about the room in wonder. He concluded that he must be dreaming, or that he had become touched in mind, or that he had died the night before and had been so happy as to get to heaven.

"At last, the Duke entered the apartment in the habit of the ducal chamberlain.

"'What will your Worship have this morning?' asked the Duke.

"The tinker stared.

"'Has your Worship no commands?'

"'I am Christopher Sly,—Sly, the tinker. Call me not "your Worship."'

"'You have not fully recovered yet, I see. But you will be yourself again soon. What suit will your Worship wear to-day? Which doublet, and what stockings and shoes?'

"Sly continued to look about him in amazement. At last, he said, with much hesitation, —

"'You may bring me my best suit. The day is pleasant. I will dress becomingly.'

"'Now you are yourself again. I must hasten to inform the Court of your recovery. I must fly to her Grace the Duchess, and say, "The Duke, the Duke is himself again!"'

"'The Duke! I tell you I am Christopher Sly, — old Sly's son, of Burton Heath, — by birth a peddler and by trade a tinker. Duke Sly! No. Duke Christopher! or, better, Duke Christophero! Marry, friend! wouldn't that sound well? It may be I am a duke, for all. Go ask Marian Hacket, the buxom inn-keeper of Wincot, if she don't know Christopher Sly, — Duke Christophero; and if she say I do not owe her fourteen pence for small ale, then call me the biggest liar and knave in Christendom!'

"The servants presently brought the poor tinker a silver basin, 'full of rose-water, and bestrewed with flowers.' Then they brought him a suit of crimson, trimmed with lace and starred. The bewildered fellow stared awhile in silence; then he slowly put on the gorgeous apparel.

"The tinker next was conducted to a magnificent banqueting-hall, where was spread a rich feast. The tables smoked with venison and sparkled with wine. He was led to a high seat beneath a canopy of silk and gold, the Duchess following, and seating herself by his side. Knights and ladies filled the tables, and the tinker began to feast and to sip wine like a duke indeed.

"'I wish'— said he, suddenly.

"'What is your wish?' asked the Duchess.

"'I wish that old Stephen Sly was here, and John Naps and Peter Turf, and my wife Joan, and Marian Hacket: wouldn't it be jolly?'

"Christopher had never smacked his lips over such wine before, and he drank so deeply that his ideas became mixed again. The feast ended The ladies sung and the musicians played, but Christopher

'Where he sleeping did snore,
Being seven times drunker than ever before.'

"And here the reign of Duke Christophero came to a sudden end. The real Duke ordered the attendants to take him away, and to put upon him his 'old leather garments again.'

"'When the night is well advanced,' said the Duke, 'take him back to the place where we found him, and there watch his behavior when he awakes.'

"Poor Christopher Sly woke in the morning to find his glory gone. The sun shone on the snow-covered gables of Bruges. He looked around him with woe in his face, as he saw the snow beneath him instead of a couch of down, and the sky above him, instead of a silken canopy, sprinkled with gold. He snuffed the frosty air, and, heaving a deep groan, he said, 'And I am old Stephen Sly's son, after all. I have seen a vision. I will go home, and take my scolding from Joan.'"

"When we visit Bruges," added Tommy, "I hope we may all visit the resting-place of Duke Christopher Sly."

Tommy's story, although not of great value to the young travellers, was loudly applauded by the Club.

"I have heard," said Wyllys, "that there is a spire in Bruges four hundred and fifty feet high, and a tower that contains forty-eight bells; but I never heard before of Duke Christopher."

Ernest Wynn, who spoke French well and took a lively interest in French poetry, sang a Norman seaside song, which is a favorite in some of the coast towns, and is especially employed by the fishermen of Etretat, when a ship goes out to sea in a storm. It began —

Le matin, quand je me réveille,	In the morn, when I awake,
Je vois mon Jésus venir,	My Jesus near I see,
Il est beau à merveille,	He is wonderfully beautiful —
C'est lui qui me réveille.	It is He that wakens me.
C'est Jésus !	It is Jesus,
C'est Jésus !	It is Jesus,
Mon aimable Jésus !	My lovable Jesus !
Je le vois, mon Jésus, je le vois	I see, I see my Jesus
Porter sa brillante croix,	Bear over the mountain high
Là haut sur cette montagne :	His cross of light, accompanied
Sa mère l'accompagne.	The Holy Mother by.
C'est Jésus,	It is Jesus,
C'est Jésus,	It is Jesus,
Mon aimable Jésus.	My lovable Jesus !

The selection was a rare one, and was mentioned by Master Lewis as being exceptionally creditable.

George Howe and Leander Towle presented acceptable exercises on " Norman Industries " and " Peasant Customs." The last topic seemed to excite Tommy Toby to try to throw some farther light on this romantic and interesting country.

"Would you like to know what lovely-looking creatures these Norman peasant girls are, and how they look ? " said he. " Well, they look [going to the blackboard and drawing with a crayon a moment] just like those."

"I am very gratified," said Master Lewis, "at the amount of historic study our proposed tour has already stimulated. One must read and study *to see*. Dr. Johnson used the comparison that 'some people would see more in a single ride in a Hempstead stage-coach than others would in a tour round the world.' Thoreau said,—

> 'It with fancy unfurled
> You leave your abode,
> You may go round the world
> By the old Marlboro' road.'

"You might have added many charming stories to those already told. In Calais, the last town of the Gallic dominions of the Plantagenets, we shall visit the scene of the siege of Edward III. and of the immortal Five who offered their lives as a ransom for their city, and whom good Queen Philippa spared. At Falaise, we may see the ruin of the castle from whose window Duke Robert, the father of the Conqueror, first saw Arletta, the tanner's daughter, and was enchanted with her beauty. At Rouen, we shall stand in the square where the Maid of Orleans was burned, and, in all places, in contrast with the dark romances of the past, will appear sunny hills, bowery valleys, and picturesque streams.

"I think it was Victor Hugo who said that 'Europe was the finest nation on the earth, France the finest country, and Normandy the finest part of France.' I do not ask you to accept his opinion, but Normandy is very beautiful."

Meetings of the Club were held every two weeks.

The boys tried to learn the secret which Tommy had been instructed to select. But he claimed that he had been instructed also to keep it.

"It would not be creditable to the Club to tell it now," he said.

CHAPTER IV.

ON THE ATLANTIC.

THE STEERAGE.—PILOT BOATS.—TOMMY MEETS ROUGH WEATHER.—HIS LETTER AND POSTSCRIPT.—QUEER PASSENGERS.—GAMES AND STORY-TELLING.—STORY OF JOAN OF ARC.—SIGNALLING AT SEA.—LAND!

AN ocean steamer! Though a speck upon the waters, what a world it seems! What symmetry, what strength, what a triumph of human skill! What a cheerful sense of security one feels as one looks upon the oak and the iron, and hears the wind whistle through the motionless forest of cordage! There society in all its grades is seen, and human nature in all its phases.

The cool upper deck of the steamer was more inviting to our tourists than the hot streets and hotels of New York, and early in the afternoon they met on the North River Pier, and went on board of their ocean home. First, they examined the elegant saloons, then their snug state-rooms, and at last the steerage apartment, where George and Leander were to have their quarters.

The steerage was not a wholly uninviting apartment. It was a plain cabin, amidships, well lighted and ventilated, and very clean. A stanch-looking pair of stairs led down to it. On each side were bunks in little rooms; those on the right hand for women, and on the left for men. These were lighted and aired by port-holes. Each passenger provided his own bedding and eating utensils.

"I like this," said Tommy Toby to the steward. "Are the passengers here more likely to be sick than in the first cabin?"

"No," said the steward. "This is the steadiest part of the ship."

"Then what is the difference between the cabin and the steerage?"

"Well, the difference is in the folks, and the furniture, and the way you eat your victuals."

The steerage passengers were allowed the freedom of the decks, but not of the grand saloons. Master Lewis and the boys seated themselves in a group on the upper deck, when they had well visited the different parts of the ship.

Early in the evening, the immense ship moved slowly and steadily away from the sultry wharves into the calm sea and cool air. The great city with its gleaming spires seemed sinking in the sea, and the hills of Neversink to be burying themselves in the shadows.

Pilot boats several times crossed the track of the steamer, with their numbers conspicuously painted on their sails.

"Why does a captain, who navigates a ship across the ocean," asked Frank of Master Lewis, " need the assistance of pilots and pilot-boats when he is in sight of land?"

"It is because the harbor is more dangerous than the open ocean, and pilots make these dangers the study of their lives.

"See yonder pilot-boat skimming with the grace of a sea-bird along the sea. It has the stanchness of a ship built for the longest voyages. It is doubtless made of the best oak, is sheathed with the best copper, and may have cost twenty thousand dollars."

"The life of a pilot must be an adventurous one," said Frank, "and there must be also much pleasure in it."

"It requires special education and hard training to become a pilot. It is expected that the candidate for the position shall have been an apprentice four years, during which he shall have performed all the duties of a common sailor, even to the washing of the decks and the tarring of the rigging. This is his college life. If he is an apt student, he then obtains a certificate of qualification from a board of commissioners by whom he has been rigidly examined.

"The pilot-boats themselves are exposed to great dangers in foggy weather. A calm comes on, and they cannot move. In this situation, they are liable to be struck by one of the great iron vessels or ocean steamers. During the last twenty-five years, some thirty pilot-boats have been lost on this coast."

PILOT-BOAT.

The night was beautiful, calm, cool, starry. In the morning, the sun rose red from the sea. Land had disappeared. The boys all met on the deck, in fine health and spirits.

Towards evening, the sea grew rough, and there were premonitions of sea-sickness among the passengers. Tommy Toby, in an amusing letter which he wrote to his parents, gave a stereoscopic pen-picture of the condition of our travellers at this period of the voyage. He afterwards added a characteristic postscript. We give Tommy's letter and postscript entire : —

MY DEAR PARENTS:

If I can only get safely back to Boston, I will never start on a voyage again. I knew it would be so. I have been seasick.
The first night and day we had very pleasant weather and a light sea.

On the evening of the second day, I was on deck with the boys. All at once the boat gave a great lurch. Then another. Then another. "We are getting into rough water," said Master Lewis.

Wyllys Wynn, who is a poet, was repeating some beautiful rhymes, when suddenly he grew white in the face, and said, "And so it goes on for several lines." He meant the poetry. Then he began to wander to and fro in search of the cabin and his state-room.

Frank Gray began to tell a story, but stopped short, and said, "The rest of it is like unto *that!*" He meant the rest of the story. Then he went to the cabin. "making very crooked steerage," one of the deck-hands said.

Ernest Wynn followed him, in the same strange gait.

"The Zigzag Club," said the deck-hand. He was a very sarcastic man.

The ship gave another dreadful lurch, and I began to feel very strange. I went to my state-room. I felt worse on the way.

The ship seemed to have lost all her steadiness.

I cannot describe the night that followed. The ship creaked, and seemed just about to roll over after every lurch. Sometimes she went up. I was so dizzy, it seemed to me that she went up almost to the moon. Then she came down. She always came down. It seemed to me she must be going down to the bottom of the sea.

In the morning, the steward came.

"It 'as been a 'eavy blow, ruther."

"A heavy blow!" said I. "Did you ever know anything like it in your life? Do you think we shall ever see land again?"

"Nothin' alarmin'," said the steward.

A dreadful day followed. I did not leave my room. I wished I had never left home I felt like the Frenchman who said, "I would kees ze land, if I could only see any land to kees."

The next day I was better, only there was a light feeling in **my head.**

I went up on deck. The sun was shining. The wind blew, but the air was very refreshing

This is the fourth day out. I have been able to eat to-day. I am feeling very hungry.

I find that all the boys have been obliged to keep their rooms, except George Howe, who is in the steerage.

How fearful I am we shall have another night like *that!* How glad I shall be to see land again! The land is the place, after all. I wish I were **sure** we would have good weather, when we return.

Your thoughtful son,

THOMAS TOBY.

P. S. Three days after. I am well now. I never felt so bright and happy in my life. The steward says that people are seldom sick twice during the same voyage. An ocean trip is just the thing, after all.

There were a few rather odd characters among the passengers: among them a portly, self-satisfied Englishman, returning from a tour of the States, with an increased respect for fine old English society; a glib-tongued Frenchman, who was delighted with "Ze States, — dee-lighted!" and whose talk was like a row of exclamation points; and a sentimental Italian fiddler, in very poor dress, going back to the beauties of Naples and the dreamy airs and skies of "Etalee."

Tommy Toby seemed to gravitate towards these people, when his sea-sickness was over.

"I likes zis American poy," said the Frenchman. "Intelegent! Has ze activitee; agilitee; very great prom-ese!"

"Our country must be very different from yours," said Tommy, one day.

"Veery, veery different indeed! Wonderful countree, — delightful! What grand rivers! what waterfalls, — Niag-e-ra! what lakes! Room for all ze world! Hospitalitee for all ze nations!"

"The Frenchman says our country is the most wonderful in all the world," said Tommy to the portly Englishman.

The latter looked very solemn; seemed about to speak, then made a long pause as though the opinion he was about to utter was a very weighty one.

"Poverty to riches, riches to poverty; now up, now down, but the animating principle always the same,— riches, riches. Wonderful people! progress! each one living to outdo the other. To-day an alderman, to-morrow in the penitentiary; to-day my Lady of Lynne, to-morrow John o' the Scales's wife!"

Tommy had an idea of what his lugubrious acquaintance meant to say, though the latter's wisdom was rather above his intellectual stature.

"We have no castles in America," said Tommy.

"Castles! No; an American family could not keep a castle: it would be sold in five years for a mill."

Tommy's face was always very bright after talking with the Frenchman, but lengthened out during the interview with his English friend. He usually retired discomforted from the latter, to seek comfort in the steerage from the lively Italian's fiddle.

There was a bright girl on board, named Agnes, — the daughter of a Boston gentleman, who was going abroad for a year. She was a social miss; witty, yet polite; speaking to every one freely, without being intrusive.

On the evening of the sixth day, nearly all the passengers were in the saloon. Agnes was asked to sing. She winningly said, —

"I will do my best, if agreeable to all." She asked to be excused a moment, and presently returned with a broad-rimmed hat and a basket, and wandering carelessly up and down the saloon sang "The Beggar Girl."

> "Over the mountain, and over the moor,
> Hungry and barefoot I wander forlorn,
> My father is dead and my mother is poor,
> And she grieves for the days that will never return.
>
> Pity, kind gentlefolk,
> Friends of humanity,
> Keen blows the blast and night's coming on;
> O give me some food
> For my mother, for charity;
> Give me food for my mother, and I will be gone."

Agnes presented her basket to one and another of the passengers, as if to solicit contributions as the song went on. All were pleased with the diversion, and it was proposed to have some other amusements during the evening.

Agnes arranged some impromptu charades: one on *Ingraciate* (in grey she ate); another on *Cowhiding* (cow hiding, in which she personated a milk-maid calling "Co boss, co boss!" and afterwards the same maid cowhiding a boy for hiding her cow). Agnes selected Tommy Toby to assist her in this last amusing tableau.

Agnes next appeared as a mind-reader. Before this last rôle, however, she was observed having a confidential chat with Tommy Toby.

"Now," said she, "if any of you are interested in clairvoyance, I shall be pleased to give an exhibition of the science. You may not know I am a mind-reader."

"She probably has been reading Master Toby's mind already," said her father, smilingly looking over his paper.

"Oh, father!"

"If each of you will write a word on a slip of paper, I will have the slips collected and put on my forehead; and I will take them from my forehead one by one, but before I take each one down, I will tell what is written upon it."

All wrote some word.

"Will some one collect the slips?" she asked.

"I will," said her father.

"I think as Thomas Toby is *spry*, I shall have to ask him to do me the favor."

"How I wish I were *spry!*" said her father.

The slips were collected. Tommy put them all on her forehead. She put up her fingers and held them there, and Tommy took a seat with his friends.

Agnes seemed in reverie. Then she said emphatically, —

"On the first slip is written 'Boston!' Who wrote that?"

"I," said Tommy Toby.

"Then it is correct?"

"Yes."

She took the slip from her forehead and laid it in her lap, saying as she did so, —

"It is not written very plainly, either."

So one by one she read all the slips. Each passenger acknowledged the writing of each announced word, after it had been correctly given by Agnes. First, the correct readings awakened wonder, then positive excitement. The experiment was repeated at the request of all, with the same wonderful result.

The diversion was reproduced on the following evening, and even Master Lewis failed to see how the girl read the slips. It was noticed however, that Tommy Toby always collected the slips, and acknowledged writing the first word. Agnes also examined each slip closely as she took it down, as if to verify the results of her very penetrating mind.

The secret of the trick was that Tommy always placed what he had written at the bottom of the slips, or last; but he acknowledged to have written what was taken from the forehead first. This gave Agnes the

JOAN OF ARC.

opportunity of reading each slip as she laid it in her lap, and of announcing what she read as though it were written on the *next* slip on her forehead.

One evening, when Master Lewis and the boys were talking of the historical places they expected to visit, Agnes approached pleasantly and said, " I have a conundrum for you."

" What is it ? " asked Master Lewis.

" What was Joan of Arc made of ? "

The boys were unable to guess.

" Suppose you tell us the story of Joan of Arc, Master Lewis," said Wyllys. " Then, perhaps, we will be able to decide."

" Yes, please," said Agnes. " I should be delighted to hear the story."

" As we expect to visit Rouen, where the Maid of Orleans "—

" I think she was Maid of " — said Tommy Toby. " I will tell you after the story."

Then Master Lewis related the story of the unfortunate shepherd girl.

STORY OF JOAN OF ARC.

" Jeanne d' Arc, known in history as the Maid of Orleans, was born in the pleasant village of Domremi, near the borders of Lorraine. Her parents were peasants, and Jeanne was their fifth child. Her education was very limited, and she spent her early years as a shepherdess.

" Her soul was full of romance and poetic inspiration, and she led a dreamy life among the flocks.

" The neighborhood of Domremi abounded in superstitions. Stories of fairies and demons, beautiful legends of the Virgin, and the mediæval traditions of the saints were the themes of fireside hours, and Jeanne drank deeply into the spirit of these wonderful myths.

" At the age of thirteen, she began to see visions and to dream dreams. She fancied that angel voices whispered in her ear, and that celestial lights flashed before her eyes.

"'At the age of thirteen,' she said, in her defence before the judge who condemned her to death, 'I heard a voice in my father's garden at Domremi, proceeding from the right on the side of the church, accompanied with a great light. At first I was afraid, but presently found that it was the voice of an angel, who has protected me ever since, who has taught me to conduct myself properly, and to frequent the church. It was Saint Michael.'

"She continued to hear strange voices. Her father said,—

"'Heed them not, Jeanne, it is but a fancy.'

"In this state of enthusiasm, she passed some five years among the vine-clad hills of Domremi, her heart estranged from worldly affections, and seeking for loving companionship from the beautiful beings that filled her dreams.

"France, at this period, was rent asunder by civil dissension, the people of the interior acknowledging Henry VI. of England as their rightful sovereign, and those of the remoter provinces, Charles VII. of France. The people of Lorraine adhered to the cause of Charles, and Jeanne became a politician in girlhood, and aspired to chivalrous deeds.

"When eighteen years of age, she fancied that celestial voices told her that she was called to deliver her country from English rule, and to place the young French king upon the throne of his fathers.

"Her father said,—

"'I tell thee, Jeanne, it is a fancy.'

"Leaving her rustic home, the unlettered girl sought an audience of Captain de Baudricourt, who commanded for Charles at Vaucoleurs. In this she was successful, and, although he at first treated her as an idle enthusiast, he was finally so impressed by the recital of her inspirations and visions, that he sent her to Chinon, where Charles held his court, to consult with the king.

"'None in the world,' she said to Baudricourt, 'can recover the

JOAN OF ARC RECOGNIZING THE KING.

kingdom of France, there is no hope but in me.' She added, 'I would far rather be spinning beside my poor mother; but I must do this work, because my Lord wills it.'

"'Who is your lord?' asked the general.

"'The Lord God!'

"'By my faith,' said Baudricourt, 'I will take you to the king.'

"She obtained an interview with Charles, whom she claimed to have recognized in a promiscuous company by a sudden inspiration, accompanied by celestial light. The story of her divine appointment deeply moved the king; and, his cause becoming desperate, he accepted the services of the fair prophetess, clad her in armor, and placed her at the head of an army of ten thousand men.

"There was something in her very appearance that inspired awe. Her mien was noble and commanding; her form was tall and elegant. She controlled her charger with wonderful grace and skill. By her side was a consecrated sword, found buried in the old church of St. Catherine de Fierbois, the existence of which she claimed to have discovered by a special revelation from above; and in her hand she carried a banner emblazoned with angels and consecrated to God.

"The English troops, with the French allies of Henry, were besieging Orleans, a famous old city, and one of the strongholds of Charles. Thither Jeanne led her army. She soon inspired her soldiers with the conviction that she held a commission from on high; and, when they arrived before Orleans, they were wrought up to the highest pitch of enthusiasm.

"Jeanne attacked the English, and in several engagements displayed superior generalship and won brilliant victories. The confidence of the French troops in her now became implicit, and they received her commands as from a messenger of celestial truth.

"The English soldiers, too, were infected by the superstition, and a panic ensued whenever she appeared. Jeanne was at last completely victorious, and, although once severely wounded, raised the siege of Orleans, and entered the city in triumph.

"The French kings for a long period had received their crowns at Rheims. The city was a great distance from Orleans, and the approaches to it were held by the English. Thither mysterious voices directed Jeanne. Charles, yielding to her influence, set out on the long and perilous journey, to be crowned in the ancient fane where his ancestors of the house of Valois had received their diadems.

"The English troops retired, and the cause of Charles received a new impetus wherever the young prophetess and her army appeared. The journey was a continued triumph for Charles, and when he reached Rheims, the fame of his success rekindled the fires of patriotism in every town and province of France.

"'It was a joyous day in Rheims of old,' when the glittering retinue, led by the young king and the peasant child, marched to the thronged cathedral. The coronation services were wonderfully impressive and inconceivably splendid. The holy unction was performed with oil said to have been brought from heaven by a dove, to King Clovis. By the side of the young monarch stood Jeanne in full armor, holding in her hand her consecrated banner. Triumphant music pealed forth, and the plaudits of the people made the old cathedral tremble. When the ceremony was over, Jeanne threw herself at the feet of the king, embraced his knees and wept.

"She felt now that her mission was accomplished. She resolved to return to her home, and to pass her days among the simple peasants of Domremi.

"But fame was too dazzling, and ambition tempted her to new exploits. She was taken prisoner at last by her enemies, the Burgundians, was delivered over to the English, put upon trial as a sorceress, pronounced guilty, and condemned to death.

"She wept over her hard fate. 'I would rather be beheaded than burned,' she said, when she reflected on the manner of her death, which was to be burned at the stake. 'Oh, that this body should be reduced to ashes!'

JOAN OF ARC WOUNDED.

"She wept for her country.

"'O Rouen, Rouen!' she said, 'is it here that I must die? Here hall be my last resting-place.'

"A huge pile of fuel was made in the ancient market place in Rouen, and the Maid of Orleans was placed upon it; and in the presnce of a vast concourse of citizens, soldiers and ecclesiastics, she was urned. Her last words were expressive of inward triumph. The mentable event occurred on the last day of May, 1431. Her ashes ere cast into the Seine, and carried to the sea.

"Joan of Arc was no wilful impostor. She fully believed that she eheld faces of departed saints, and heard the voices of beings from the nseen world. The result of her wonderful career was that Charles ltimately won back to the royal house of Valois the whole kingdom of rance.

"An imposing mausoleum in the city of Orleans perpetuates her emory; but her name stands above mortality, independent of marble r bronze. Apart from her character as a visionary, Jeanne was a most oble girl. The French still cherish an enthusiastic attachment for er memory, and a yearly fête is given in honor of her deeds in the ity of Orleans."

"I think," said Tommy Toby, "that I can answer Agnes's conunrum. Joan of Arc was Maid (made) of Orleans."

"Right," said Agnes. "What an agreeable company the Zigzag lub is!"

One afternoon the man on the lookout called the attention of those ound him to a distant object: it seemed like a mere speck in the orizon. He presently said,—

"It is a ship."

The news spread. Every one came upon deck. Even the cooks the galley left their pots and kettles.

As she drew near, the British ensign was seen fluttering at the ern. As she drew still nearer, she hoisted five small flags.

Then one of the quartermasters on our own ship brought several small flags and a signal-book from the wheel-house. He opened the book to a page of colored pictures of small flags, five of which corresponded to those raised by the ship in view. Opposite each flag was a figure. The figures combined in order made the number 94,362.

The quartermaster turned to another page, and opposite this number appeared the name and port of the ship.

The ship hoisted another set of flags, which was answered by our own ship.

"She asks to know our reckonings," said the quartermaster.

"Can a ship meeting another ask other questions in this way?" inquired George Howe.

"Oh, yes; two vessels miles apart can carry on a long conversation with each other. Ships have a regular alphabet of signal flags."

"What are signals of distress?" asked George.

"That flag," said the quartermaster, pointing to a picture in the book, "means a fire or a leak. (1)

"This means a want of food. (2)

"And that, aground. (3)

"Here is one that signifies, 'Will you take a letter from me?'" (4)

This dialogue between the two ships was the most pleasing and exciting episode of the voyage, until land began to appear as a dim streak upon the horizon.

CHAPTER V.

THE LAND OF SCOTT AND BURNS.

GLASGOW. — VISIT TO AYR. — STORY OF HIGHLAND MARY. — GLASGOW TO EDINBURGH. — SCENE IN EDINBURGH AT NIGHT. — THE CASTLE. — MELROSE. — LONG SUMMER DAYS.

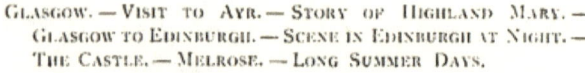

OLD Glasgow, almost encircled by hills and uplands, presents a picturesque view, as the steamer moves slowly up the narrowing channel of the Clyde. But with its rapid commercial growth, its 2,000,000 spindles, its steam-power, and its busy marts of trade, it is a city of the present rather than the past, and beyond the Knox monument and the cathedral presents few attractions to the history-loving stranger.

Our tourists stopped at Glasgow to make a day's excursion to the home of Burns. They were taken from the boat to the Queen's Hotel in George's Square; but George Howe and Leander Towle, after resting with the rest of the party, secured lodgings in a private house.

The boys arose the next morning, with dreams of the Doon and Ayr. To their disappointment, a heavy mist hung over the city; and they found it a dreary and disappointing walk to the South Side Station, where they were to take the train for Ayr. The two hours' ride on the train was as colorless; they were whirled through a novel and beautiful summer landscape, but Nature had dropped her sea-curtain and sky-curtain of fog and mist over all.

The barometer, too, wore a cloudy face, and frowned at them, as though it meant never to predict fine weather again.

But, after waiting awhile at the station, there were signs of lifting clouds and clearing skies. A weather-wise old Scotchman promised the party a fair day, and bid them "God speed" for the home of "Robb Burns." Presently, the sun began to shoot his lances through the mist and the tourists set out for their first walk, which was to be a two-mile one to Burns's cottage.

BIRTHPLACE OF ROBERT BURNS.

The cottage was indeed an humble one. It was built by the father Burns, with his own hands, before his marriage, and originally con- ined two rooms.

In the interior of the kitchen, a Scotchwoman showed to the party ecess where

"The bard peasant first drew breath."

The simplicity of the place and its ennobling associations seemed to ech all except Tommy, who remarked to Frank Gray, —

"I was born in a better room than that myself."

"But I fear you never will be called to sing the songs of a nation."

"I fear I never shall," said Tommy, meekly.

From the cottage, the party went to the Burns monument. From the base of its columns, the beauties of Scottish scenery began to appear.

"It is the way in which one ends life that honors the place of one's birth," said Frank to Tommy.

"So I see," said Tommy, as the sun came out and covered the beautiful monument, and illuminated the record of the poet's fame.

The tourists, under the direction of a Scottish farmer, whose acquaintance Master Lewis had made, next proceeded to an eminence commanding a view of the mansion house of Coilsfield, the romantic haunting Castle of Montgomery.

"There," said the Scotchman, "lived Burns's first sweetheart."

"Highland Mary?" asked several voices.

"Yes."

"They were separated by death," said Master Lewis. "Can you tell us the story?"

"As Mary was expecting soon to be wedded to Burns, she went to visit her kin in Argyleshire. She met Burns for the last time on a Sunday in May. It was a lovely day, and standing one on the one side and one on the other of a small brook, and holding a Bible between them, they promised to be true to each other for ever.

"On the journey, Mary fell sick and died. You have read Burns's lines 'To Mary in Heaven'?"

> That sacred hour can I forget?
> Can I forget the hallowed grove,
> Where by the winding Ayr we met,
> To live one day of parting love?
> Eternity will not efface
> Those records dear of transports past;
> Thy image at our last embrace!
> Ah! little thought we 'twas our last!

"Do you ever sing the songs of Burns?" asked Master Lewis.

"Would you like to hear me try 'Highland Mary'?"

"Do!" said Ernest Wynn, who was always affected by ballad music.

The Scotchman quoted a line or two of the poem, changing from the English to the Scottish accent. The boys were charmed with the words, and sat down on the grass to listen to

HIGHLAND MARY.

>Ye banks and braes and streams around
>   The castle o' Montgomery,
>Green be your woods, and fair your flowers,
>   Your waters never drumlie!
>There simmer first unfauld her robes,
>   And there the langest tarry :
>For there I took the last fareweel
>   O' my sweet Highland Mary.
>
>How sweetly bloomed the gay green birk,
>   How rich the hawthorn's blossom,
>As underneath their fragrant shade
>   I clasped her to my bosom!
>The golden hours, on angel wings,
>   Flew o'er me and my dearie ;
>For dear to me as light and life
>   Was my sweet Highland Mary.
>
>Wi' monie a vow, and locked embrace,
>   Our parting was fu' tender :
>And, pledging aft to meet again,
>   We tore oursels asunder :
>But, oh ! fell death's untimely frost
>   That nipt my flower sae early !
>Now green 's the sod, and cauld 's the clay,
>   That wraps my Highland Mary !
>
>Oh, pale, pale now, those rosy lips,
>   I aft hae kissed sae fondly !
>And closed for aye the sparkling glance
>   That dwelt on me sae kindly !
>And mould'ring now in silent dust
>   That heart that lo'ed me dearly !
>But still within my bosom's core
>   Shall live my Highland Mary.

The "banks and braes and streams around" gleamed like a vision of enchantment in the full noon sunlight. Never had the boys listened to a song amid such highly romantic associations.

Bidding the entertaining Scotchman farewell, the party returned to Ayr, and thence to Glasgow, where it arrived in the lingering sunlight of the long afternoon.

The next morning it left by rail for Edinburgh, that city of high houses and terraced hills; of grandly picturesque beauty; of the time of Bruce, and the bright and dark days of the Stuarts; where one is surrounded by the relics of a thousand years, and stands under the protecting shadow of a castle that seems lifted into the region of air.

The party took rooms on Prince's Street, a thoroughfare one hundred feet wide and a mile in length, graced with noble monuments of art and bowery pleasure-grounds. It is considered one of the most picturesque streets in the world.

Around you are shops with splendid windows, statues, public gardens, birds, and flowers; above you are houses six or eight stories high; above these, on the rocky hillsides, are queer old buildings of other times; and high over all is the Castle, cold and grand on its rocky throne.

"I shall rest to-morrow, boys," said Master Lewis, "and shall let you roam at will. Let us spend the evening in one of the public gardens."

After supper, the party went to one of these fragrant street-gardens. The band of the Duchess of Sutherland's Own, as a certain Highland regiment is called, filled the quiet air with delicious music.

The sun withdrew his light from the street, the gardens, and the tall houses on the hills, but the Castle stood long in the mellowed glory of the sunset.

But the sun left even the Castle at last, and then began a spectacle that seemed like an illusion or fairy-land.

Lights began to twinkle in the streets; then in the tall windows

EDINBURGH CASTLE

above them. Now and then a whole face of an antique pile was illuminated; now some little eyrie that seemed hanging in air burst into flame; now a line of terraces began to twinkle. The lights crept up the hillsides everywhere.

"I never saw any thing so beautiful!" said Ernest Wynn.

Every one talks of the Castle in Edinburgh, and the boys paid their first visit to it, and saw it in its morning glory. On the highest platform of the Castle, three hundred and eighty-three feet above the sea, stands the celebrated old cannon Mons Meg, made in Mons, in Brittany, in 1486. It had figured in so many wars and historic scenes, that the Scottish people came to regard it as a national relic. The site of the Castle is about seven hundred feet in circumference, and on three sides it seems just a bare rock, rising almost perpendicularly in air.

The boys next visited Arthur's Seat, a high rock on the top of a hill, in which there is a fancied resemblance to a chair. Queen Victoria

HOLYROOD PALACE.

MARY STUART.

climbed up to it on a recent visit. It commands a sweeping view of the sea, and the hills that encircle the city.

They next went to the old Palace of Holyrood, and were shown the apartments of the unfortunate Queen of Scots.

"There," said the tall Scotchman who attended them about the place, "is the room where Rizzio was murdered, in the presence of Mary."

They were told that a certain stain in the floor was the blood of the hapless man.

"We must ask Master Lewis to tell us the whole story," said Wyllys.

They next visited St. Giles, the scene of the preaching of Knox, the Martyrs' Monument, and Knox's grave.

"We must have an evening meeting of the Club in Edinburgh," said Willis Wynn, when the party with Master Lewis were at tea.

"To-night?" asked Frank.

"I would wait until after we have been to Abbotsford," said Master Lewis. "Then I would have a meeting in the parlor, and let each one tell some story associated with the most interesting object he has seen."

The next day Master Lewis and the tourists, except George and Leander, who preferred remaining in the city, took the train for Mel-

MURDER OF RIZZIO

rose, stopped at Melrose Station, and rode to Abbotsford, the reputed haunt of Thomas the Rhymer, and the residence of Walter Scott.

They were met at the entrance of the gray mansion by a tall Scotchman, and were taken from the magnificent entrance hall, about forty feet in length, to the dining-room, which has a wonderful black-oak roof, and is the place where Sir Walter died. Gazing from the window on the beautiful landscape for the last time, he said to Lockhart, " Bring me a book." " What book ? " " There is but one book."

They were next shown the library, a repository of some twenty thousand books and of presents from most eminent persons, among them a silver urn from Lord Byron and two arm-chairs from the Pope.

Our tourists next visited the ruin of Melrose Abbey, and found it less interesting than its historic associations. Late evening found them again in Edinburgh.

"What time of the evening do you think it is?" asked Master Lewis of the boys as they entered the hotel.

" Seven o'clock," said Tommy Toby.

" After nine o'clock," said Master Lewis.

The Castle still stood in the damask light of the twilight, like a dark picture on an illuminated curtain.

" The summer days in these Northern regions are as long as they are beautiful," said Master Lewis.

CHAPTER VI.

STORY TELLING IN EDINBURGH.

STORY OF QUEEN MARY AND RIZZIO. — STORY OF THE BLACK DOUGLAS. — STORY OF A GLASGOW FACTORY BOY. — THE CASTLE BY MOONLIGHT.

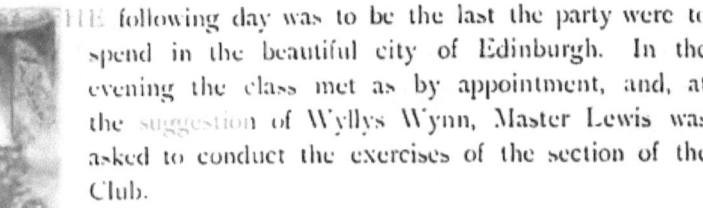

THE following day was to be the last the party were to spend in the beautiful city of Edinburgh. In the evening the class met as by appointment, and, at the suggestion of Wyllys Wynn, Master Lewis was asked to conduct the exercises of the section of the Club.

"I thank you," he said, "for this kind confidence, and I think we may congratulate ourselves on the success of our journey thus far. I will begin our conversation by asking Wyllys Wynn what is the most interesting place he has seen in Scotland."

"The place that has most excited my interest," said Wyllys, "is the room in the palace where Rizzio was killed. It is not the most interesting place I have seen, of course, but it has most awakened my curiosity."

"Will you not tell us the history of Rizzio?"

"To do so," said Master Lewis, "would require some account of the whole of Queen Mary's life. The romance of Queen Mary's story will have a freshness, after what you have now seen. I will do the best I can to relate those incidents which make up the

STORY OF QUEEN MARY AND RIZZIO.

"Mary, Queen of Scots, was perhaps the most beautiful in person and winning in manners and polite accomplishments of any modern queen. She was the daughter of James V. of Scotland and Mary of Lorraine. Her father heard of her birth on his death-bed. He had hoped his heir would prove a son.

"'It came with a lass, and it will end with a lass,' said he.

"The crown of Scotland came with the daughter of Bruce, and ended with unfortunate Mary.

"Mary became queen before she was a week old. Little she knew, in her innocent cradle at Linlithgow, of the crown waiting her head or the kingdom that was ruled in her name.

"Her childhood was like a fairy story. She had three Marys for playmates, as she herself was named Mary; and each Mary was the daughter of a noble family.

"When six years of age she was given in marriage to Francis II., the son of the French King. The French fleet carried her away from the rugged shores of Scotland, and the Scottish Marys went with her.

"Ten years were passed amid the gayeties and splendors of the French court, and then, at the age of sixteen, she was married, amid great pomp and rejoicings, to the Dauphin, whose courtly devotion and elegant society she had long enjoyed. The associations of the young pair before marriage had been very happy. They delighted to be with each other even in society, when they would often separate themselves from the gay throngs around them.

"The next year found Francis on the throne, and Mary seemed to be the happiest queen in the world.

"But the following year the young king died, childless, and Mary was compelled to return to Scotland.

"Mary was a Catholic. Scotland had adopted the Reformed Faith, and the Scots received her with coldness and suspicion.

"Mary's life from childhood to her imprisonment was a series of romances associated with marriage schemes. Francis had not been long dead before many of the courts of Europe were planning marriage alliances with the beautiful Queen. The kings of France, Sweden, Denmark, Don Carlos of Spain, the Archduke of Austria, and many others of lesser rank were named as suitable candidates for her hand.

"Her own choice fell upon her handsome cousin, Lord Darnley, who was a Catholic, and among the nearest heirs to the English crown. He was a weak, corrupt, ambitious man. But he had a winning face, and the marriage was celebrated in Holyrood Palace, in the summer of 1565.

"One day, long before this marriage, as Mary was coming down the stairs of the Palace, she saw the graceful form of a dark Italian musician reclining on a piece of carved furniture in the hall. It was her first view of David Rizzio, who had come to Scotland in the train of the embassador from Savoy. In a celebrated picture of Mary, she is represented as starting back in surprise and horror at the sight of this adventurer, as though the moment were one of fate and evil foreboding.

"This fascinating Italian won the confidence of Mary by his arts, and used his influence to bring about the marriage with Darnley. He became a friend of Darnley; they occupied the same apartments and engaged in the same political intrigues.

"But, after the marriage, Rizzio himself drew away the affections of the Queen from Darnley, who determined to assassinate Rizzio. Several Scottish lords united with Darnley to do the deed.

"One day, when Mary had been supping with Rizzio, the white face of Lord Ruthven appeared at the door of the room.

"'Let *him* come out of the room,' he said to the Queen.

"'He shall not leave the room,' said the Queen; 'I read his danger in your face.'

"Then Ruthven and his followers rushed upon Rizzio, dragged him from the room, and stabbed him fifty-six times. You have seen the bloodstains in the Palace, where the wily Italian was killed.

"It is said that his body was thrown upon the same chest, at the foot of the stairs, where Mary had seen him first.

"Mary knew that Darnley had caused the murder.

"'I will now have my revenge,' she said, in the presence of the conspirators.

"She said to Darnley, 'I will cause you to have as sorrowful a heart as I have now.'

"For political reasons she, however, became seemingly reconciled to him. Three months after the tragedy, James VI. of Scotland and I. of England was born. You have seen his birthplace to-day.

"Twelve months passed. Earl Bothwell, a profligate noble, had won the Queen's confidence. There is little doubt that the two formed a plot to destroy Darnley's life.

"The Queen went to visit Darnley at Glasgow, he having fallen ill. She pretended great affection for him, and brought him to Edinburgh, and secured lodgings for him in a private house. She left him late one Sunday evening, to attend a marriage feast.

"She remarked to him, in one of their last interviews, —

"'It was about this time, a year ago, I believe, that David was murdered.'

"After she had gone, there was a great explosion, and Darnley's dead body was found in a neighboring garden.

"Mary had had her revenge.

"Three months after the tragedy she married Bothwell, who had secured a divorce from his young wife to prepare the way for the event.

"Scotland rose against Mary. She fled to England, and threw herself on the protection of Elizabeth, abdicating the throne in favor of her son. She was secured as a prisoner, and confined at Carlisle. She was taken from Carlisle to Fotheringhay Castle. She was at last tried

FRANCIS II. AND MARY STUART LOVE-MAKING.

or conspiracy against the life of Elizabeth. Sentence of death was passed upon her. She protested her innocence. You know the rest, —the last tragedy of all, in the Castle of Fotheringhay.

"Bothwell died an exile and a madman, some nine years after his marriage with Mary.

"It is said that it was found, after her execution, that her real hair, under her wig, was as white as that of a woman of seventy. I cannot wonder.

"She had one little friend who remained true to the last. It was her little dog. He followed her to the block, and cowered, frightened, under her dress, at the fatal moment, and lay down beside her headless body when the last tragedy was over. It could not be driven away from its mistress; and when the body was removed it began to droop, as though understanding its loss, and in two days it died."

"I have spoken at school a poem by Bulwer Lytton, founded on the incident," said Wyllys.

"Can you now repeat it?" asked Master Lewis.

"I will try."

THE DEAD QUEEN.

The world is full of life and love: the world methinks might spare,
From millions, one to watch above the dust of monarchs there.
And not one human eye! — yet, lo! what stirs the funeral pall?
What sound — it is not human woe wails moaning through the hall.
Close by the form mankind desert one thing a vigil keeps:
More near and near to that still heart it wistful, wondering, creeps.
It gazes on those glazèd eyes, it hearkens for a breath:
It does not know that kindness dies, and love departs from death.
It fawns as fondly as before upon that icy hand,
And hears from lips that speak no more the voice that can command.

To that poor fool, alone on earth, no matter what had been
The pomp, the fall, the guilt, the worth, the dead was still a Queen.
With eyes that horror could not scare, it watched the senseless clay,
Crouched on the breast of death, and there moaned its fond life away.
And when the bolts discordant clashed, and human steps drew nigh,

The human pity shrank abashed before that faithful eye;
It seemed to gaze with such rebuke on those who could forsake.
E'en turn'd to watch once more the look, and strive the sleep to wake.
They raised the pall, they touched the dead: a cry, and *both* were stilled,
Alike the soul that hate had sped, the life that love had killed.

Semiramis of England,¹ hail! thy crime secures thy sway;
But when thine eyes shall scan the tale those hireling scribes convey,
When thou shalt read, with late remorse, how one poor slave was found
Beside thy butchered rival's corse, the headless and discrowned,
Shall not thy soul foretell thine own unloved, expiring hour,
When those who kneel around the throne shall fly the falling tower? —
When thy great heart shall silent break; when thy sad eyes shall strain
Through vacant space, one thing to seek, one thing that loved — in vain?
Though round thy parting pangs of pride shall priest and noble crowd,
More worth the grief that mourned beside thy victim's gory shroud!

Master Lewis continued the general subject of the meeting.

"What, Frank, has been the most interesting object you have seen?"

"The Cannongate. I read its history in the guide-book, and I spent an hour in the place. One could seem in fancy to live there hundreds of years."

"King James rode through this street on his way to Flodden," said Master Lewis. "Montrose was dragged here upon a hurdle. It was in a church here that Jenny Geddes bespoke the sentiment of the people by hurling her stool at the head of the Dean, who attempted to enforce the Episcopal service.

"'I will read the Collect,' said the Dean.

"'Colic, said ye? The De'il colic the wame of ye!'

"Here came John Knox, after his interview with Queen Mary, cold and grim, and unmoved by her tears. Here rode the Pretender. Here dwelt the great Dukes of Scotland and the Earls of Moray and Mar."

"I wished I were a poet, a painter, or an historian, when I was there," said Frank. "It is said Sir Walter Scott used to ride there

¹ Elizabeth.

THE DEATH-BED OF FRANCIS II.

slowly, and that almost every gable recalled to him some scene of triumph or of bloodshed."

"I cannot begin to tell you stories of Cannongate," said Master Lewis. "Such stories would fill volumes, and give a view of the whole of Scottish history. What, Ernest, has impressed you most?"

"The view of Edinburgh at night is the most beautiful sight I have seen. But the charm that Scott's poetry has given to Melrose Abbey, haunts me still, notwithstanding my disappointment at the ruin. This was the tomb of the Douglases and of the heart of Bruce.

"I will tell you a story of one of the Douglases, whose castle still stands, not far from Melrose," said Master Lewis; "a story which I think is one of the most pleasing of the Border Wars. I will call the story

THE BLACK DOUGLAS.

"King Edward I. of England nearly conquered Scotland. They did not have photographs in those days, but had expressive and descriptive names for people of rank, which answered just as well. So Edward was known as 'Longshanks.' It was from no lack of spirit or energy that he did not quite complete the stubborn work; but he died a little too soon. On his death-bed he called his pretty, spiritless son to him, and made him promise to carry on the war; he then ordered that his body should be boiled in a caldron, and that his bones should be wrapped up in a bull's hide, and carried at the head of the army in future campaigns against the Scots. After these and some other queer requests, death relieved him of the hard politics of this world, and so he went away. Then his son, Edward II., tucked away the belligerent old King's bones among the bones of other old kings in Westminster Abbey, and spent his time in dissipation among his favorites, and allowed the resolute Scots to recover Scotland.

"Good James, Lord Douglas, was a very wise man in his day. He may not have had long shanks, but he had a very long head, as you shall presently see. He was one of the hardest foes with whom the two Edwards had to contend, and his long head proved quite too powerful for the second Edward, who, in his single campaign against the Scots, lost at Bannockburn nearly all that his father had gained.

"The tall Scottish Castle of Roxburgh stood near the border, lifting its grim turrets above the Teviot and the Tweed. When the Black Douglas, as Lord James was called, had recovered castle after castle from the English, he desired to gain this stronghold, and determined to accomplish his wish.

"But he knew it could be taken only by surprise, and a very wily ruse it must be. He had outwitted the English so many times that they were sharply on the lookout for him.

"How could it be done?

"Near the castle was a gloomy old forest, called Jedburgh. Here, just as the first days of spring began to kindle in the sunrise and sunsets, and warm the frosty hills, Black Douglas concealed sixty picked men.

"It was Shrove-tide, and Fasten's Eve, immediately before the great Church festival of Lent, was to be celebrated with a great gush of music and blaze of light and free offerings of wine in the great hall of the castle. The garrison was to have leave for merry-making and indulging in drunken wassail.

"The sun had gone down in the red sky, and the long, deep shadow began to fall on Jedburgh woods, the river, the hills, and valleys.

"An officer's wife had retired from the great hall, where all was preparation for the merry-making, to the high battlements of the castle, in order to quiet her little child and put it to rest. The sentinel, from time to time, paced near her. She began to sing, —

'Hush ye, Hush ye,
Hush ye, Do not fret ye
Little pet ye; The Black Douglas
Hush ye. Shall not get ye.'

MARY STUART SWEARING SHE HAD NEVER SOUGHT THE LIFE OF ELIZABETH.

"She saw some strange objects moving across the level ground in the distance. They greatly puzzled her. They did not travel quite like animals, but they seemed to have four legs.

"'What are those queer-looking things yonder?' she asked of the sentinel as he drew near.

"'They are Farmer Asher's cattle,' said the soldier, straining his eyes to discern the outlines of the long figures in the shadows. 'The good man is making merry to-night, and has forgotten to bring in his oxen; lucky 't will be if they do not fall a prey to the Black Douglas.'

"So sure was he that the objects were cattle that he ceased to watch them longer.

"The woman's eye, however, followed the queer-looking cattle for some time, until they seemed to disappear under the outer works of the castle. Then, feeling quite at ease, she thought she would sing again. Spring was in the evening air; it may have made her feel like singing.

"Now the name of the Black Douglas had become so terrible to the English that it proved a bugbear to the children, who, when they misbehaved, were told that the Black Douglas would get them. The little ditty I have quoted must have been very quieting to good children in those alarming times.

"So the good woman sang cheerily.—

> "'Hush ye.
> Hush ye.
> Little pet ye!
> Hush ye.
>
> Hush ye.
> Do not fret ye:
> The Black Douglas
> Shall not get ye!'

"'DO NOT BE SO SURE OF THAT!' said a husky voice close beside her, and a mail-gloved hand fell solidly upon her shoulder. She was dreadfully frightened, for she knew from the appearance of the man he must be the Black Douglas.

"The Scots came leaping over the walls. The garrison was merry-making below, and, almost before the disarmed revellers had any warn-

> "Hush ye,
> Hush ye,
> Do not fret ye;
> The Black Douglas
> Shall not get ye!"

It is never well to be too sure, you know.

"Douglas had caused his picked men to approach the castle by walking on their hands and knees, with long black cloaks thrown over

THE BLACK DOUGLAS SURPRISING AN ENEMY.

their bodies, and their ladders and weapons concealed under their cloaks. The men thus presented very nearly the appearance of a herd of cattle in the deep shadows, and completely deceived the sentinel, who was probably thinking more of the music and dancing below than of the watchful enemy who had been haunting the gloomy woods of Jedburgh.

"The Black Douglas, or 'Good James, Lord Douglas,' as he was called by the Scots, fought, as I have already said, with King Robert Bruce at Bannockburn. One lovely June day, in the far-gone year of 1329, King Robert lay dying. He called Douglas to his bedside, and told him that it had been one of the dearest wishes of his heart to go to the Holy Land and recover Jerusalem from the Infidels; but since he could not go, he wished him to embalm his heart after his death, and carry it to the Holy City and deposit it in the Holy Sepulchre.

"Douglas had the heart of Bruce embalmed and inclosed in a silver case, and wore it on a silver chain about his neck. He set out for Jerusalem, but resolved first to visit Spain and engage in the war waged against the Moorish King of Grenada. He fell in Andalusia, in battle. Just before his death, he threw the silver casket into the thickest of the fight, exclaiming, 'Heart of Bruce! I follow thee or die!'

"His dead body was found beside the casket, and the heart of Bruce was brought back to Scotland and deposited in the ivy-clad Abbey of Melrose.

"Douglas was a real hero, and few things more engaging than his exploits were ever told under the holly and mistletoe, or in the warm Christmas light of the old Scottish Yule-logs."

"What has interested you most in Scotland," said Master Lewis to George Howe, continuing the subject.

"I am hardly interested in antiquities at all," said George, frankly. "I try to be, but it is not in me. A living factory is more to my taste than a dead museum. The most interesting things I have seen are the great Glasgow factories. As for stories, I have been thinking of one that has more force for me than all the legends I ever read."

"We shall be glad to hear you tell it," said Master Lewis. "My business is teaching, and it is my duty to stimulate a love of literature.

But I have all respect for a boy with mechanical taste; no lives promise greater usefulness. We will listen to George's story."

"It is not a romantic story," said George. "I will call it

A GLASGOW FACTORY BOY.

"Just above the wharves of Glasgow, on the banks of the Clyde there once lived a factory boy, whom I will call Davie. At the age of ten he entered a cotton factory as 'piecer.' He was employed from six o'clock in the morning till eight at night. His parents were very poor and he well knew that his must be a boyhood of very hard labor. But then and there, in that buzzing factory, he resolved that he would obtain an education, and would become an intelligent and a useful man. With his very first week's wages he purchased 'Ruddiman's Rudiments of Latin.' He then entered an evening school that met between the hours of eight and ten. He paid the expenses of his instruction out of his own hard earnings. At the age of sixteen he could read Virgil and Horace as readily as the pupils of the English grammar schools.

"He next began a course of self-instruction. He had been advanced in the factory from a 'piecer' to the spinning-jenny. He brought his books to the factory, and placing one of them on the 'jenny,' with the lesson open before him, he divided his attention between the running of the spindles and rudiments of knowledge. He now began to aspire to become a preacher and a missionary, and to devote his life in some self-sacrificing way to the good of mankind. He entered Glasgow University. He knew that he must work his way, but he also knew the power of resolution, and he was willing to make almost any sacrifice to gain the end. He worked at cotton-spinning in the summer, lived frugally, and applied his savings to his college studies in the winter. He completed the allotted course, and at the close was able triumphantly to say, '*I never had a farthing that I did not earn.*'

"That boy was Dr. David Livingstone."

"An excellent story," said Master Lewis. "A sermon in a story, and a volume of philosophy in a life. Now, Tommy, what is the most attractive thing *you* have seen?"

"I see it now. Oh, look! look!" said Tommy, flying to the window.

The full moon was hanging over the great castle, whitening its grim turrets.

The boys all gazed upon the scene, which appeared almost too beautiful for reality.

"It looks like a castle in the sky," said Wyllys.

Story-telling was at an end. So the exercises ended with an exhibition of Edinburgh Castle by moonlight.

CHAPTER VII.

A RAINY EVENING STORY AT CARLISLE.

The Druids and Romans. — The Story of the Jolly Harper Man. — "When first I came to Merry Carlisle."

"CARLISLE!" said Master Lewis, as the cars stopped at a busy looking city, the terminus of many lines of railway.

"Carlisle?" asked Frank Gray, glancing at the evidences of business energy about the station. "Carlisle? I have heard that the city was a thousand years old."

"An old city may grow," said Master Lewis, on the way to the hotel. "In 1800, Carlisle had but 4,000 inhabitants, now it has more than 30,000."

Carlisle was the ancient seat of the kings of Cambria, and was a Roman station in the early days of the Christian era. It was destroyed in 900 by the Danes, was ravaged by the Picts and Scots, was doubtless visited by Agricola, Severus, and Hadrian, and it has a part in the history of all the Border wars. Here half-forgotten kings lived; here Roman generals made their airy camps, and near it the grotesque ships of Roman emperors dropped their sails in the Solway. Here Chris-

ROMANS INVADING BRITAIN.

ianity made an early advent, and the hideous rites of the Druid priests disappeared.

The ancient Druids worshipped in sacred groves; the oaks were their fanes and chapels, but they erected immense stone temples open to the sky, the moon, and stars: these were their cathedrals. In them were great stones used as altars of sacrifice, and on their altars the dark and mysterious priests offered up human victims to their gods.

The country around Carlisle abounds in Roman and Druidical relics, and in antiquities associated with the Border contests. At Penrith may be seen the ruins of a Druid temple, formed of sixty-seven immense stones, called "long Meg and her daughters."

The Isle of Man, the ancient and poetic Mona, whose grand scenery was once the supposed abode of the gods of the Saxons, lies near the Solway, and to it excursion steamers go from the western coast towns of England carrying pleasure seekers all the long summer days. Here

the Druids gathered after the defeat of the Saxons by the Romans, and thither the Romans followed them, and fell upon the long-bearded priests and the wild torch-bearing priestesses, and put them to the sword. The island of Mona may be called the Druid's sepulchre.

The afternoon was rainy, and the boys though impatient, were confined to the hotel.

In the evening Master Lewis said, —

"One of the most quaint and curious of old English ballads is associated with Carlisle and is founded upon a funny story which illustrates the rude simplicity of the early English court. The ballad may be found in the Percy Society's Collections, which you may some day examine in the Boston Public Library, or indeed in any great library at home or in England. It is entitled 'The Jolly Harper Man.' I will relate it to you in the rather decorated style that I once heard it told to a company of young people at a Christmas gathering in one of the London charity schools. I hope it will interest you as much now as it did the boys and girls who listened to it then.

DRUID SACRIFICE

THE STORY OF THE JOLLY HARPER MAN AND HIS GOOD FORTUNE.

"Many, many years ago, — as long ago as the days of Fair Rosamond, when Henry Plantagenet and his unruly family governed England, and some think as long ago as old Henry I., — there lived in Scotland a jolly harper man, who was accounted the most charming player in all the world. The children followed him in crowds through the streets, nor could they be stopped while he continued playing; even the animals in the woods sat on their haunches to listen when he wandered harping through the country; and the fair daughters of the nobles immediately fell in love as often as he approached their castles.

"King Henry had a wonderful horse — a very wonderful horse — named *Brownie*. He did not quite equal in dexterity and intelligence the high-flying animal of whom you have read in the 'Arabian Nights,' but he knew a great deal, and was a sort of philosopher among horses, — just as Newton was a philosopher among men. King Henry said he would not part with him for a province, — he would rather lose his crown. In this he was wise, for a new crown could have been as easily made as a stew-pan; but all the world, it may be, could not produce such another intelligent horse.

"King Henry had fine stables built for the animal, — a sort of horse palace. They were very strong, and were fastened by locks, and bars, and bolts, and were kept by gay grooms, and guarded day and night by soldiers, who never had been known to falter in their devotion to the interests of the king.

"So strongly was the animal guarded, that it came to be a proverb among the English yeomanry, that a person could no more do this or that hard thing than 'they could steal Brownie from the stables of the king.'

"The king liked the proverb; it was a compliment to his wisdom and sagacity. It made him feel good, — so good, in fact, that it led him one day quite to overshoot the mark in an effort that he made to increase the people's high opinion.

"'If any one,' said he, after a good dinner, — 'if any one were smart enough to get Brownie out of his stables without my knowledge, I would forgive him for his cleverness, and give him an estate to return the animal.' Then he looked very wise, and felt very comfortable and very secure. 'But,' he added, 'evil overtake the man who gets caught in an attempt to steal my horse. Lucky will it be for him if his eyes ever see the light of the English sun again.'

"Then the report went abroad that the man who would be so shrewd as to get possession of the king's horse should have an estate, but that he who failed in the attempt should lose his head.

"The English court, at this time, was at Carlisle, near the Scottish border. The jolly harper man lived in the old town of Striveling, since called Stirling, at some distance from the border.

"The jolly harper man, like most people of genius, was very poor. He often played in the castles of the nobles, especially on festive occasions; and, as he contrasted the luxurious living of these fat lords with his own poverty, he became suddenly seized with a desire for wealth, and he remembered the proverb, which was old even then, that 'Where there is a will there is a way.'

"One autumn day, as he was travelling along the borders of Loch Lomond, a famous lake in the middle of Scotland, he remembered that there was a cave overlooking the lake from a thickly wooded hill, in which dwelt a hermit, who often was consulted by people in perplexity, and who bore the name of the 'Man of Wisdom.'

"He was not a wicked magician, nor did he pretend to have any dealings with the dead. He was gifted only with what was called clearness of vision; he could see into the secret of things, just as Zerah Colburn could see into difficult problems of mathematics, without study. Things that were darkness to others were as clear as sunlight to him. He lived on roots and herbs, and flourished so wonderfully on the diet, that what he didn't know was considered not worth knowing.

"It was near nightfall when the jolly harper man came to the famous hill. The sun was going down in splendor, and the moon was coming

THE HERMIT.

up, faint and shadowy, and turning into gold as the shadows deepened. Showers of silver began to fall on Loch Lomond, and to quiver over the valleys. It was an hour to fill a minstrel's heart with romantic feeling, and it lent its witchery to the heart of the jolly harper man.

"He wandered up the hill overlooking the lake, where dwelt the

Man of Wisdom to whose mind all things were clear. He sat down near the mouth of the cave, partook of his evening meal, then, seizing his harp, began to play.

"He played a tune of wonderful sweetness and sadness, so soft and airy that the notes seemed to glide down the moonbeams, like the tinkling of fairy bells in the air. The wicked owl pricked up his ears to listen, and was so overcome that he wished he was a more respectable bird. The little animals came out of the bushes, and formed a circle around the jolly harper man, as though enchanted.

"The old hermit heard the strain, and came out to listen; and, because he had clearness of vision, he knew that music of such wonderful tenderness could be produced only by one who had great gifts of nature, and who also had some secret longing in his heart.

"So he came up to the jolly harper man, walking with his cane, his gray beard falling over his bosom, and his long white hair silvered in the moonlight.

"The jolly harper man secretly expected him, or at least he hoped that he would come out. Like the Queen of Sheba, he wished to test the wisdom of this new Solomon, and to inquire of him if there were no way of turning his wonderful musical genius into bags of gold.

"'Why do you wander here, my good harper?' asked the hermit, when the last strain melted away in low, airy echoes over the lake. 'There are neither lads to dance nor lassies to sing. This hill is my dominion, and the dominion of a hermit is solitude.'

"'See you not Loch Lomond silvered in the moon?' said the jolly harper man. 'Nature inspired me to touch my harp, and I love to play when the inspiration of Nature comes upon me.'

"The answer pleased the hermit as much as the music.

"'But why is your music so sad, my good harper man; what is there that you would have that fortune denies?'

"'Alas!' said the jolly harper man, 'I am very poor. My harping all die in the air, and leave me but a scanty purse, poor clothing, and no roof over my head. You are a man of wisdom, to whom all things are clear. Point out to me the way to fortune, my wise hermit. I have a good liberal heart; you could not do a service to a more deserving man.'

"The old hermit sat down on a stone in silence, resting his chin on his staff. He seemed lost in profound thought. At last he looked up, and said slowly, pausing between each sentence, —

"'Beyond the border there is a famous country; in that country there is a palace; near the palace there is a stable, and in that stable there is a stately horse. That horse is the pride of the kingdom; the man who would get possession of that horse, without the king's knowledge, might exchange him for a province.'

"'Wonderful! wonderful! But —'

"'Near Striveling town there is a hill; on the hillside is a lot; in the lot is a fine gray mare, and beside the gray mare is a foal.'

"'Yes, yes! wonderful! but —'

"'I must now reveal to you one of the secrets of Nature. Separate that mare from the foal, though it be for hundreds of miles, and, as soon as she is free, she will return to her foal again. Nature has taught her how, just as she teaches the birds of passage the way to sunny islands; or the dog to find the lost hunter; or —'

"'Yes, yes; all very wonderful, but —'

"'In your hand you carry a harp; in the harp lies the power to make merry; a merry king makes a festive board, and festivity produces deep sleep in the morning hours.'

"The jolly harper man saw it all in a twinkling; the way to fortune lay before him clear as sunlight. Perhaps you, Tommy, do not get the idea so suddenly. If not, I fear you are not gifted like the good hermit with clearness of vision.

"The jolly harper man returned to Striveling the next day, after spending the night with the hermit on the borders of Loch Lomond.

"The following night he was summoned to play before two famous Scottish knights, Sir Charles and Sir Roger. They were very valiant, very rich, and, when put into good humor, were very liberal.

"The jolly harper man played merrily. The great hall of the castle seemed full of larks, nightingales, elves, and fairies.

"'Why, man,' said Sir Roger to Sir Charles, in a mellow mood, 'you and I could no more harp like that than we could gallop out of Carlisle on the horse of the king.'

"'Let me make a prophecy,' said the jolly harper man at this. 'I will one day ride *into* Carlisle on the horse of the king, and will exchange the horse for an estate.'

"'And I will add to the estate five ploughs of land,' said Sir Roger; 'so that you never shall lack for a home in old Scotland.'

"'And I will add to the five ploughs of land five thousand pounds,' said Sir Charles; 'so that you never shall lack for good cheer.'

"The next morning the jolly harper man was seen riding out of Striveling town on a fine gray mare; but a little colt was heard whinnying alone in the high fenced lot on the side of the hill.

"It had been a day of high festival at Carlisle; it was now the cool of the summer eve; the horn of the returning hunter was heard in the forest, and gaily plumed knights and courtiers were seen approaching the illuminated palace, urging their steeds along the banks of the river Eden, that wound through the moonlit landscape like a ribbon of silver.

"The feast was at its height. The king's heart was merry. There only needed some novelty, now that the old diversions had come to an end, to complete the delights of the festive hours.

"Suddenly sweet sounds, as of a tuning harp, were heard without the palace. Then music of marvellous sweetness seemed to fill the air. The windows and doors of the palace were thrown open. The king himself left the table, and stood listening on the balcony.

"A merry tune followed the airy prelude; it made the nerves of the old nobles tingle as though they were young again; and, as for the king, his heart began to dance within him.

"'Come in! come in, my harper man!' shouted the king, shaking his sides with laughter, and patting a fat noble on the shoulder with delight. 'Come in, and let us hear some more of your harping.'

"The jolly harper man bowed very low. 'I shall be glad to serve your grace; but first, give me stabling for my good gray mare.'

"'Take the animal to my best stables,' said the king. ''Tis there I keep my Brownie, the finest horse in all the land.'

"The jolly harper man, accompanied by a gay groom, then took his horse to the stables; and, as soon as he came out of the stable-door, struck up his most lively and bewitching tune.

"The grooms all followed him, and the guards followed the grooms. The servants all came flocking into the hall as the jolly harper man entered, and the king's heart grew so merry, that all who came were made welcome, and given good cheer.

"The small hours of night came at last, and the grand people in the hall began to yawn, one after another. The jolly harper man now played a very soothing melody. The king began to yawn, opening his mouth each time a little wider than before, and finally he dozed off in his chair, his head tilted back, and his mouth stretched almost from ear to ear. The fat nobles, too, began to snore. First the king snored, and then the nobles, which was a very proper way of doing the thing, — the blissful sound passing from nose to nose, and making a circuit of the tables.

"The guards, grooms, and servants began to feel very comfortable, indeed; and, though it was their business to keep awake, their eyelids grew very heavy, and they began to reason that it would be perfectly safe to doze while their masters were sleeping. Who ever knew any mischief to happen when everybody was asleep?

"The jolly harper man now played his dreamiest music, and just as the cock crew for the first time in the morning, he had the satisfaction of seeing the last lackey fall asleep. He then blew out the lights, and crept nimbly forth to the stables. He found the stable door unlocked, and the gray mare kicking impatiently about, and whinnying for her foal.

"Now, what do you suppose the jolly harper man did? Guess, if you have Clearness of Vision. He took from his pocket a stout string, and tied the halter of the king's horse, the finest in all the land, to the halter of his own animal, and patting the fine gray mare on her side said: 'And now go home to your foal.'

"The next morning all was consternation in the palace. The king's horse was gone. The king sent for the jolly harper man, and said,—

"'My horse has escaped out of the stables, the finest animal in all the land!'

"'And where is my fine gray mare?' asked the jolly harper man.

"'Gone, too,' said the king.

"'I will tell you what I think,' said the jolly harper man, with wonderful confidence. 'I think that there has been a rogue in the town.'

"The king, with equal wisdom, favored the idea, and the jolly harper man made an early escape that morning from the palace.

"Then the jolly harper man went as fast as he could to Striveling. Of course, he found his fine gray mare in the lot with her foal, and the king's horse tied to her halter; and, of course, he rode the noble animal into Carlisle; and presenting himself before the two knights, Sir Roger and Sir Charles, claimed his five ploughs of land and five thousand pounds.

"'Go to! go to!' said Sir Roger, pointing at him in derision; and Sir Charles laughed a mighty laugh of scorn. 'The man does not live who could ride away the king's Brownie! Go to!'

"'The king's Brownie stands in your own court!' cried the jolly harper man; and Sir Roger and Sir Charles paid their forfeits without another word.

"Then the jolly harper man returned the king's horse to the royal owner: and who ever heard of such a thing as a king breaking his promise? Not the jolly harper man, you may be sure."

"Is the story a true one?" asked Tommy Toby.

"The story, as I heard it, was acknowledged to be considerably embellished; and I have tried to make it as attractive as possible. You should always remember this, that a good historic story gathers color by time. The stories of Faust, Macbeth, King Lear, William Tell, Robert the Devil, and many others I might name, have but meagre facts for a starting point."

"I know a story of Nottingham, that I think as funny as that," said Tommy. "It is about the Wise Men of Gotham."

"We will hear it when we go to Nottingham," said Master Lewis. "I think we will go there at once, after an excursion to the English Lakes."

The next morning George Howe and Leander Towle left the party for Birmingham, London, and Paris, as their means would not admit of their making easy zigzag journeys through England, in the way that Master Lewis had planned for the other boys. They agreed to meet Master Lewis and their companions in London, on their return from Paris, at which time they would have completed their tour, and would be obliged to leave for home before the others made their journey through Normandy.

Ernest Wynn, as we have said, was very fond of old English and Scottish ballads, and he never lost any good opportunity to hear a new song.

While the party were talking over their plans for visiting English places, the sound of a piano in an adjoining room fell upon Ernest's ear.

He left his companions, and, going into the open room from which the music came, listened attentively to the playing.

"Do you sing?" asked Ernest of the player, who was a pleasant-faced little miss about ten or twelve years of age.

"Sometimes."

"I like music. Will you not sing for me?"

"If I can. What would you have me sing?"

"Oh, something about Carlisle; something that I would not hear at home."

"Where is your home?"

"In America."

"In America! What, so far? Perhaps you would like to hear 'Mona's Waters?'"

"Yes," said Ernest.

The song was very winningly sung.

"Now perhaps you would like to hear 'When first I came to merry Carlisle'?"

Ernest smiled.

"It doesn't mean you at all. It was a girl who lost her lover in one of the Border Wars.

"'When first I came to merry Carlisle,
Ne'er was a town sae sweetly seeming:
The white rose flaunted o'er the wall,
The thistled banners far were streaming.

"'When next I came to merry Carlisle,
Oh sad, sad, seemed the town, an' eerie!
The auld, auld men came out and wept,
O maiden! come ye to seek yere dearie?'"

"Thank you for that song," said Ernest. "I have heard 'Highland Mary' sung at Ayr, and shall always remember it. And I shall also be pleased to recollect,—

"'When first I came to merry Carlisle.'"

"And 'the girl I left behind me,'" said Tommy Toby to Ernest softly.

The Miss saw the point of the joke, and, as it was politely spoken, received the implied compliment with becoming modesty and good humor, saying that she should also remember very pleasantly the visit of the Zigzag Club to her father's house.

CHAPTER VIII.

A CLOUDLESS DAY.

SHERWOOD FOREST. — NOTTINGHAM. — STORY OF THE WISE MEN OF GOTHAM.

"HAVE stood by the graves of Wordsworth and Coleridge. The trees were green and cool; the Rotha rippled beside the poets' resting-place, and Helvellyn and Catchedicam in the distance rose in the calm, bright air. Beautiful indeed are these mountains in midsummer. The whole Lake region is beautiful — beautiful!"

Such was the brief entry Wyllys Wynn made in the journal in his guide-book, on returning from the English Lakes.

"There is a touching story associated with Helvellyn," said Wyllys to Master Lewis, as the boys were returning from the Lakes, "that Scott has told in very musical verse. It is of a little dog that watched beside the dead body of his master for several months, and was found guarding the bones. Will you not relate it to us?"

"Wordsworth and Scott, I think," said Master Lewis, "both tell the story in verse.

"About the year 1805 there dwelt in the district a young man of elegant tastes, who loved to explore these mountain regions. He was well known for his literary attainments, and greatly beloved for his gentle and amiable manners.

"He used to make frequent excursions among the wild mountains, and would spend whole days feasting his eye on the exhaustless beauties they afforded. He was always attended by a little terrier dog, to which he was greatly attached, and which was ever on the alert to do his master's bidding. Scott, in his ballad, calls the young man the Wanderer, and so I will call him now.

"One spring day, when the streams were swollen, and the mountains were all alive with waterfalls, birds, and flowers, the Wanderer set out on an excursion that promised unusual attractions, attended by his little favorite. He penetrated too far, or remained too long; night probably overtook him, and he lost his way. He fell from a precipice, and was dashed in pieces. For several months the little dog watched by the remains of his beloved master, only leaving them, it is supposed, to obtain necessary food. The remains of the Wanderer were found during the following summer by a party of excursionists, and, when discovered, the terrier was guarding them with pitying care.

"Sir Walter Scott, in company with Wordsworth, ascended Helvellyn during the following autumn, and visited the spot where the Wanderer died. The well-known ballad, one of the most pathetic of Scott's poetical compositions, was the result of this excursion.

"'I climbed the dark brow of the mighty Helvellyn,
Lakes and mountains beneath me gleamed misty and wide,
All was still, save by fits, when the eagle was yelling,
And starting around me the echoes replied.
On the right Striden-edge round the Red tarn was bending,
And Catchedicam its left verge was defending,
One huge, nameless rock in the front was ascending,
When I marked the sad spot where the Wanderer had died.'"

The Class stopped at Sheffield, and thence began their first experience of English stage-coaching to the old town of Mansfield. They entered the latter upon a market-day, and found the streets full of empty carts, cattle, and rustic people, presenting a scene of truly ancient simplicity. Mansfield is still a miller's town, and must present nearly the same appearance as in the days of Henry II., who, according to the old ballad, was lost in the forests near the place. The forests, however, have changed: little remains of them but a heath, traversed by wild and romantic roads. Here and there a great tree, like a forest lord, may be seen, to remind one of the kingly hunting days.

Leaving Mansfield for Sherwood Forest, strange houses by the wayside, excavated in limestone and recalling the supposed age of the cave-dwellers, as in an unexpected picture, much excited the boys' curiosity.

Sherwood Forest, or as much of it as remains, is twenty-five miles long and about eight broad. The new growth of trees is very fine; but it is the remains of the grand old oaks that attract the tourist and summer wanderer. The wood has a ground-work of exhaustless ferns, the delicate birches flutter in the warm winds, their peculiar shade contrasting with the greenery around them. Here and there oaks of different ages and altitudes rise gray, gnarled, and almost leafless, — oaks on which a thousand tempests have beaten, and around which ten thousand storms have blown. In Henry II.'s time not only Nottingham, but the whole of England, was covered with oaks.

Tommy Toby was very urgent to visit some of the old historic oaks of Sherwood, especially such as are associated with saint stories and tragic histories.

SHAMBLE OAK.

Procuring a guide, the Class went first to see Shamble Oak. Think of it: in the main circuit it is thirty-four feet! It is called Shamble Oak because a butcher once used its hollow trunk to conceal stolen sheep. He was hung on an oak.

The guide next took the boys to a dreamy old place called Welbeck Park, to see the Greendale Oak, supposed to be seven hundred years old, and which has a circumference of more than thirty-five feet!

"It looks as though it had the rheumatism," said Tommy. "With all of its crutches and canes it will not live many years longer. Do you think it will?"

"I think it likely to out live all of us," said the guide. "More than one hundred and fifty years ago an arch was cut in this tree, and a lord rode through it on his wedding day. It was very, very old then; but the lord is gone and the oak lives."

GREENDALE OAK.

The guide procured for the party a vehicle, and drove to Parliament Oak, under which it is said that Edward I. held a Parliament in 1290. The tree still furnishes green boughs. Its girth is about twenty-nine feet.

Newstead Abbey, the home of Lord Byron, forms a part of the old forest of Sherwood, and is but a short distance from Mansfield. It was founded by Henry II., and presents one of the picturesque and interesting ruins in this part of England.

"You will not be allowed to visit the Abbey," said the guide. "The rooms of Lord Byron remain just as he left them; his bedstead, with gilded coronets, his pictures, portraits of friends, writing-table, and all; but it is private property, and visitors are not allowed."

"The Abbey was built by Henry as one of the many peace offerings which he made for the murder of Thomas à Becket," said Master Lewis. "You remember the story?"

"Yes," said Wyllys Wynn. "Thomas à Becket claimed

PARLIAMENT OAK.

that the power of the clergy was superior to the power of the king, and Henry pronounced him a traitor. He was killed at the altar by a party of conspirators, whose deed had the supposed sanction of the king. Henry did penance at Thomas à Becket's tomb."

"He stripped his back, and allowed the monks to whip him, did he not?" said Tommy. "I remember the picture of it in my history."

Distant views of Newstead, so full of strange memories and fantastic histories, were all the Class could obtain. The ruin looked down upon the charming old Nottinghamshire woodlands like a picture of the past, and the spirit of romance and poetry seemed to linger around it still.

Going next to the fine old town of Nottingham, almost the first thing which the boys desired to see was Mortimer's Hole. This is a

MORTIMER'S HOLE.

passage through a sand-rock, more than three hundred feet in length. Through this passage young Edward entered Nottingham Castle by night, and thus surprised and captured Mortimer (Earl of March). The wicked Earl was conveyed by the same passage out of the castle so secretly that the guards were not aware that it had been entered.

In the evening spent at Nottingham, Tommy Toby was asked about his story of which he had spoken in connection with the place.

MURDER OF THOMAS À BECKET

"It is not a story of Nottingham, but of Gotham, near Nottingham. It is about the Wise Men."

"Who went to sea in a bowl?" asked Frank.

"No, they were much wiser than that. I will try to tell it in the way Master Lewis tells his stories: in the rather *decorated* style."

"I hope you will always have as nice a sense of honor as you show now," said Master Lewis, "whenever you make the slightest change from plain truth to parable. You have a tact for story-telling, for one so young; and you studied up the story of 'The Frolicsome Duke,' which you told the Club, in a manner that quite surprised us. I hope this story will prove as entertaining."

THE STORY OF THE WISE MEN OF GOTHAM.

"More than six hundred and fifty years ago, there reigned in England a king, named John. They called him *Sansterre* or Lackland, for, unlike his brothers, he had received from his father no fiefs.

"He was the son of Henry Plantagenet, a good king, as kings went in those rude times, who governed England for thirty-four years.

"His mother was Eleanora of Aquitaine, who was, in her day, the prettiest girl in France. But she was a wilful little woman and full of craft. She married the French king first, but, not liking him on account of his monkish ways, she procured a divorce, and told Henry Plantagenet, who was young and handsome and gay, that she would like to marry him. He accepted the proposal, because the union would add to his dominions several provinces. Henry loved Rosamond Clifford, — 'Fair Rosamond,' — whom he had met in the valley of the Wye, and who was the prettiest girl in all the world.

"The marriage proved an unhappy one. Henry soon discovered what a wily, wilful little woman she was; he tried to curb her, and a terrible time he had.

"Richard succeeded his father. It was he who made the grandest crusade of the Middle Ages; who was married at Cyprus in flower-time; who fought with noble **Saladin** at Acre and **Jaffa**; **who** was obliged to sail away from **the** Holy Land; who looked back **from** his beautiful ship on **the** unconquered coast with regret; who was shipwrecked and cast upon **a** hostile coast; and who was discovered, when imprisoned in a gloomy old castle on the Danube, by the **harp** of Blondel the Troubadour.

"Then came John, in whose veins flowed **the** worst blood **of** King Henry's family. Prince Arthur, Geoffrey's **son, had the** best claim to the crown, but somehow **John** got himself crowned, **and he** began to reign so terribly that the hearts of the barons quaked within **them ; and so,** for a time, he silenced all opposition. He was **as cunning as bad** Queen Eleanora, and he loved to make mischief **as well.** He would order that a man should be killed, apparently with **as little** conscience **as** he would have ordered a butcher **to slay a sheep. Most bad** kings have been notable for **some good qualities ; King John, so far** as I know, had none.

"In Nottinghamshire there is an **old town, removed** from the great centres of life and activity, called Gotham. **The** inhabitants were of good Saxon stock, **and they hated the whole race of** Norman Plantagenets. These people **had** learned something **of** liberty from bold Robin Hood, 'all under **the** greenwood tree.'

"One day there came a report to Old Gotham **that King John** was making a progress, and would pass through the **town. Now it was** an old custom in feudal times that the course **that a king** took, in passing for the first time through a district or a **shire, should** become ever after a public highway. The people of Gotham wanted **no** public highway to their town, **no avenue** that would open **their retreat** to the Normans, and put **them** more easily **in the** power of **brutal kings. And they** hated John. So they **held a council, and** resolved that the feet of John Lackland, the murderer, should never dishonor the town of Gotham.

"But the people understood that it would **be a** foolhardy work to oppose the progress **of** the king openly. They must rely upon their

RICHARD'S FAREWELL TO THE HOLY LAND.

wits. The men decided to go in a body and fell large trees across a certain upland, over which the royal party must pass to enter the town. This they did, making a barrier through which mounted horsemen would find it difficult to break, and which would compel a party like the king's to turn off by another way.

"When King John came to the eminence, and found his progress arrested, he was very angry, and, finding a couple of rustics near the place, he demanded of them who had made the barrier.

"'The people of Gotham,' answered one of the rustics.

"'Go you to Gotham,' said the king, 'and tell the people from me, that as soon as I return to camp I will send a troop to cut off their noses.'

"The two rustics ran off, terribly frightened, and reported the cheerful intelligence at Gotham. Oh, then there were stirring times in that old town! The people had no wish to receive a kingly decoration in that way.

"What was to be done?

"They met for consultation.

"Now there were wise men in Gotham, and, when the convention met, these wise men expressed their opinions not only on the nose question, but on public affairs in general. After a long deliberation, one of these wise men, whom I will call Fitz Peter, said: 'Our wits have thus far prevented King John from setting foot in our town, and our wits are able to save our noses.' This opinion was received with great satisfaction.

"But how should they accomplish the end?

"Now chief among the wise men of Gotham was one whom I will call Leofric. He at last stood up with a very knowing look, and said: 'I have heard of many people who were punished for being wise, but I never heard of a person who was punished for being a fool. When the king's troops come, let us each imitate a safe example, and act like a fool.'

"At this the people shouted. So they decided to rely on their wits for the safety of their noses, and to act like fools.

"One morning, very early, as a party of horsemen were leaving the town for hunting, a troop appeared, with a fierce sheriff at their head.

"The bowmen were terribly scared, and the question passed around as to what they should do. They hit upon a plan, and threw away their hunting-gear. When the sheriff came up, he found the old men rolling great stones up the hill, and the young men bending over and grunting as if they were in great distress.

"'What are you doing?' demanded the sheriff of one of the old men who was tugging away at a stone.

"'We are rolling stones up hill for day.'

"'You old fool!' said the sheriff. 'Go home and go to bed, and day will come itself.'

"'Why,' returned the man, as though greatly astonished, 'I never thought of that. How wise you be! You are the wisest man I ever did see!'

"'And what are you doing?' asked the sheriff, of one of the young men.

"'We do the *grunting*,' was the prompt reply.

"'The old men do the lifting, and the young men do the grunting!' exclaimed the sheriff. 'Well,' he added, in sudden good-humor, 'that is the way the world goes everywhere!' And he galloped away, leaving the men unharmed.

"The sheriff next met four old women, with brooms on their shoulders.

"'Whither away?' asked the sheriff.

"'To the priest's, to be married,' said they all.

"'To the priest's, to be married?'

"'We go every morning to be married,' answered one of the old crones, 'and we have been for the last forty years!'

"'Then why are you not married?'

"'The priest says that we do not bring the right thing. We carry something new every morning.'

"'But why do you not take a *man*?'

"'A MAN!' exclaimed the old woman, leaping straight into the air. 'A MAN? I never thought of that! How wise you be! Why, you are the wisest man that I ever did see!'

LIMESTONE DWELLINGS.

"The sheriff next met some men who had started on a journey, each of whom carried on his back a door.

"'Why do you carry that door?' asked the sheriff of one of the travellers.

"'Left my money at home.'

"'Then why not leave the door at home too?'

"'Afraid of thieves.'

"'Afraid of thieves? Then leave your door at home to protect your money.'

"'They can't break in, because, you see, I've got the door.'

"'Leave your door at home, and take your money with you.'

"'I never thought of that. How wise you be! You are the wisest man that I ever did see!'

"The sheriff let the travellers pass on unmolested.

"'The people are all fools here,' he said.

"'It would be too bad to harm such simple people,' said his comrades.

"'Fools all,' said the sheriff.

"'Fools all,' said the horsemen.

"'Let us go back,' said the sheriff, 'and report to the king that the people in Gotham are fools.'

"'Right,' said the men.

"So they returned to the king, and reported that Gotham was a place of fools. And from these circumstances, or incidents like these, if I may believe an old tale, the men of that place were called, in derision, 'The Wise Men of Gotham,' from that day."

CHAPTER IX.

A SERIES OF MEMORABLE VISITS.

TOMMY GOES HUNTING. — "PEVERIL OF THE PEAK." — THE BOY AT THE WHEEL. — LEAMINGTON. — STRATFORD-ON-AVON. — SHAKSPEARE'S BIRTHPLACE, GARDEN, AND TOMB. — QUEER RELICS. — KENILWORTH. — ERNEST'S ALBUM OF LEAVES AND FLOWERS. — WARWICK CASTLE. — THE MIGHTY GUY. — THE ANTIQUE PORTRESS.

MASTER LEWIS gave the boys a couple of days in Nottingham to enjoy themselves as they liked.

Tommy Toby went *hunting*.

"I want to be able to tell people," he said, "that I have hunted in Sherwood Forest, the royal hunting-ground of English kings."

"In midsummer?" asked Master Lewis. "I fancy if you were to use a gun in the Forest of Sherwood, you might make a longer vacation abroad than you intended."

"I do not intend to use a gun. I have bought me a bow and some arrows."

"Let me see them," said Master Lewis. "They look very harmless, certainly." Master Lewis seemed to hesitate about making further objections.

Just what came of Tommy's hunting we cannot state at this stage of our narrative. He left the boys at the hotel, bow and arrows in hand, and saying as a word of parting, —

"'Let's go to the wood, said Richard to Robin.'"

He evidently went outside of the city into the wooded district, that was a part of old Sherwood Forest. When Master Lewis found that he had really gone out of the place he looked troubled, and said:—

"I should have prevented it."

Tommy returned late on the evening of the same day after a ten hours' absence. He certainly looked like a modern hunter, for he was empty handed, and his clothes were in a very disarranged condition.

"Where are your bow and arrows?" asked Frank.

"I shall tell you nothing at all about it, now," said Tommy. "It is my own secret."

"Then you have two secrets," said Frank, referring to the fact that Tommy had been made custodian of the secret he was supposed to have selected for the Club."

"Yes, but *that* don't *amount to much*," said Tommy.

"*Nothing, after all,*" said Master Lewis, quietly, who had seen Tommy's conundrum on a card. "I did not suppose that you really intended to spend the day in the country alone with bow and arrow."

"Just look at my legs," said Tommy, rolling up his pants, and showing bloody scars.

"Where did you get *them?*" asked Master Lewis.

"*Up a tree.* Please do not ask me now. If you will excuse me from telling you now, I will give you a full account some other time."

"I will excuse you from giving an account of yourself, to-night; but please remember that you must not go hunting, or anywhere, alone again without my permission," said Master Lewis, noticing some singular rents in Tommy's clothes.

Tommy went to his supper.

"I've been chased by the *terriblest* bull you ever saw," he whispered confidentially to Wyllys Wynn, as he passed him. "I'll tell you all about it some time."

He added, —

"And that ain't all. I've been chased by *John* Bull, too."

Ernest Wynn went, under an arrangement made for him by Master Lewis, to the Peak near Castleton, wishing to view the scene of Sir

PEVERIL OF THE PEAK.

Walter Scott's charming romance, "Peveril of the Peak." He found here only a pitiful ruin, and instead of knights with dancing plumes and silver shields, with which fancy pictures the eyry of the grand old Norman baron, he met some very strange-looking mining people, who are often to be seen in the rural districts in this part of England.

One incident touched Frank's kind heart, and seemed more to

impress him than the associations of manorial splendor he had made the journey to see.

In the entrance of one of the caves of the Peak was a little rope-spinner, who was lame, and whose time was spent from sun to

THE BOY AT THE WHEEL.

sun in turning the wheel, — always the same, faithfully turning the wheel.

"I gave him a shilling," said Frank. "spoke kindly to him, and left him gazing after me with tears in his eyes, still turning his wheel, turning his wheel."

From Nottingham Master Lewis and the boys went to Birmingham, and Frank Gray and Ernest Wynn made a détour to the little village of Madeley, and visited Boscobel, the place of refuge of King Charles II. after his defeat at the battle of Worcester. The king first arrived at White Ladies about three-quarters of a mile from Boscobel House: there he secreted himself in an oak, afterwards famous as the Royal Oak of Boscobel. The brothers Penderell, foresters and yeomen, concealed him in closets in their simple mansion, being true to their sovereign, at the risk of their lives, when it might have raised them from poverty to riches to have uttered a treacherous word.

BOSCOBEL.

The closets in which Charles was concealed are exhibited to visitors, and Frank and Ernest were allowed to pass up and down the passages that had afforded so secure a retreat to the fugitive. In the parlor they were shown a chimney-piece, and on one of the panels a picture of the king in the oak, and on another the king in disguise on horseback, escorted by the Penderells.

It is said that the king's pursuers were thrown off the right track of discovery by an owl that flew out of the oak where he was concealed, leading the captain to say, "The owl loveth not company, and where he is no one else can be." It is also related that when Charles complained of the slowness of the horse on which he fled in disguise, one of the Penderells remarked that the animal never before had "the weight of three kingdoms on his back." These stories may not be quite true, but one is reminded of them by the figures on the chimney-piece.

KING CHARLES'S HIDING PLACE

The Class next went to Leamington, a most convenient point from which to make short excursions to Stratford-on-Avon, Warwick Castle, and Kenilworth Castle. Leamington, although itself not historically interesting, is provided with excellent hotels, being an English watering-place.

The first excursion of the party from Leamington was to Stratford-on-Avon, to the house where Shakspeare was born, and the church in which he was buried.

The birthplace of Shakspeare is an antique-looking stone house two stories high, with picturesque gables fronting the street. In the room where he first saw the light of the world he was to enrich with his thought there is a cast of his face taken after his death, and a portrait painted in the prime of his life. The latter showed a truly noble brow; it was such a face as fancy itself might paint, so royally did seem endowed with genius. In this room Sir Walter Scott had in

SHAKSPEARE.

scribed his name on a pane of glass, and Wordsworth once wrote a stanza which is still preserved under glass. It began with these lines : —

> "The house of Shakspeare's birth we here may see ;
> That of his death we find without a trace.
> Vain the inquiry, for immortal he" —

Here the poet seemed to pause as though the literary work was not satisfactory; he drew his pen across what he had written, and under it wrote the following stanza : —

> "Of mighty Shakspeare's birth the room we see ;
> That where he died, in vain to find we try.
> Useless the search, for, all immortal be ;
> And those who are immortal never die."

The effort furnishes a curious illustration of the methods of a poet's mind in careful composition.

Back of the house is a garden, in which grew the old English flowers that are portrayed by the poet in his dramas.

From the house the party went to the cottage of Anne Hathaway, Shakspeare's wife, whom he loved in youth when life's bright ways lay fair before him. It is a house which is mainly noticeable for its simplicity.

"There is the place where he sat when he came to see his sweetheart," said the old lady who showed the house.

Shakspeare and his wife sleep in the same beautiful church amid the bowery town of Stratford-on-Avon; and thither, rowing up the Avon almost to the churchyard, our tourists made their way.

The party approached the church through an avenue of limes, and entered the richly-carved oak doors of the Gothic porch. The tomb of Shakspeare is in the chancel. The Avon runs but a short distance from the walls, and the cool boughs of the summer trees wave before the windows. A flat stone marks the place where the poet is buried, on which are inscribed the oft quoted lines said to be written by the poet himself : —

> " Good friend, for Jesus' sake forbear
> To dig the dust enclosèd here!
> Blest be the spade that spares these stones,
> And curst be he that moves my bones."

Over the grave, in a niche of the wall, is a bust of the poet. The inscription mentions his age as fifty-three years.

Returning to the birthplace, Frank Gray and Tommy Toby visited the Shakspeare Museum. The collection of curiosities was some-

RUINS OF KENILWORTH CASTLE.

Tommy showed a great contempt for Frank's wonder-talk.

"I've found something now," he said, "that outdoes all the rest. It is a letter written — "

"By Shakspeare?" asked Frank, in an animated way.

"No: *to* Shakspeare."

"By whom?"

"Mr. Richard Quyney. You have often heard of him, I suppose?"

"He was probably a literary man," said Frank.

"Probably. He asked for a *loan* of thirty pounds."

The next day's trip was to Kenilworth Castle, an ivy-hung ruin associated with the whole of England's history, and traditionally with the romances of King Arthur. The walls are broken, the great banqueting hall has just fallen into decay, and where the coronals flashed and astrals blazed at night, now shine only the dim light of the moon and stars. Here Queen Elizabeth was entertained by her favorite; the Earl of Leicester. The splendor of that reception has rarely been equalled. The fête, which was one long banquet, broken by a most wonderful series of dramatic representations, lasted seventeen days. There were tilts and tournaments; the park was peopled with gods and goddesses to surprise the Queen wherever she went; nymphs and mermaids rose from the pools, and there was minstrelsy on every hand. Thirty-one barons were present. Ten oxen were slaughtered every morning, sixteen hogsheads of wine and forty hogsheads of beer were consumed daily. There were lodged in the castle four hundred servants, all of whom appeared in new liveries of velvet, and shared the unrestrained hospitality.

"All the clocks in the castle were stopped during that long festival," said Master Lewis, "and the hands were all left pointing at the banquet hour."

"But time went on," said Wyllys Wynn.

"Yes, time went on, and the maiden Queen grew old as all mortals must, and there came a time when her vanity could no longer be deceived. She sought to keep from sight the white hairs and wrinkles of age by every art, but Nature did its work, as with Canute and the sea. When her form and features began to lose whatever of beauty they once possessed, she tried to banish from her mind the reality that she was past her prime by viewing herself in false and flattering mirrors.

"But the wrinkles grew deeper, and the white hairs multiplied, and her limbs lost their power, and her strength at last was gone. Her flatterers still fed her fondness for admiration with their arts, and while life offered her any prospect she still smiled upon those whom she must have suspected were deceiving her.

"'One day,' says her attendant, Lady Southwell, 'she desired to see a *true glass*, which in twenty years before she had not seen, but only such an one as on purpose was made to deceive her sight.'

"They brought it to the poor withered Queen. She raised it to her face with her bony hands, and looked. For the first time for years she saw herself.

"It was a revelation. Her old rage came back again. She pointed to her flatterers with scorn, and ordered them to quit her presence.

"Then came the Archbishop of Canterbury, disgracing his sacred office by his words. 'Madam,' said he, 'your piety, your zeal, and the admirable work of the Reformation afford great grounds of confidence for you.'

"But the wretchedly disenchanted woman could no longer be deceived.

"'My lord,' she said, 'the crown that I have borne so long has given me enough of *vanity* in my time. I beseech you not to augment it at this hour.

"She had seen herself, and the world also, in the true glass."

Ernest Wynn was observed by Master Lewis making a collection of ivy leaves at Kenilworth.

"Do you collect leaves at all the historic places you visit?" he asked.

PORTRAIT OF ELIZABETH.

"I picked some heather at the birthplace of Burns, brought ivy from Melrose, and wild flowers from Newstead and from the Peak, and I purchased flowers from Shakspeare's garden."

"What do you intend to do with them?"

"I will tell you privately. George Howe is pleased with collections of interesting things, — shells, stamps, autographs. He has but little money, and I am making a scrap-book of pictures, leaves, and flowers collected at notable places, as a present for him."

"It seems to me an admirable plan," said Master Lewis. "I should be pleased with such a book myself."

The next day the party visited Warwick Castle, one of the finest and best preserved of all the ancient country seats of the English nobility. To one approaching it, its rich lawns, its towering trees (of which some are from Lebanon), its picturesque windows, and harmony of design make it an ideal of castellated beauty.

The Class was ceremoniously admitted by men in livery, and was taken charge of by a portly and pompous Englishwoman, who wore a black silk that rustled as she swept along. She carried a bunch of keys at her side, and evidently entertained a high sense of the dignity of her position.

"*This*," said the stately lady, pointing to an immense structure of armor, "this is the armor of the mighty Guy."

"The mighty Guy!" said Tommy Toby, with large eyes, "will you please tell us who *he* was?"

The antique portress stared as though amazed at such a confession of ignorance.

"We are from America," said Tommy.

Master Lewis smiled at being included in the uninstructed "we."

"Guy was a giant."

Tommy's interest grew.

"He was the great Earl of Warwick: a valiant soldier who slew so many people that he became melancholy, and retired to Guy's

Cliff, as it is now called, and there lived alone in a cave for thirty years. He was *nine* feet high."

"And what is *that?*" said Tommy Toby, pointing to an immense pot.

"That," said the antique lady, "was the mighty Guy's *porridge pot.*"

"How much does it hold?"

"It holds one hundred and twenty gallons, and weighs eight hundred pounds."

"Did the mighty Guy drink as much porridge as that at every meal?" asked Tommy, his curiosity taking a wider circle with each new statement.

"I don't know; all of these things happened long, long before I was born."

"*That,*" said the lady, "is a rib of the Dun Cow."

"What kind of a cow was that?" asked Tommy.

"It was a cow which the mighty Guy killed on Dunsmore Heath. It weighs nine pounds and a half."

"The cow?"

"No, the rib."

The lady led the party in a procession which she dramatically headed through the lower rooms of the principal building. She showed them the superb old baronial hall; the drawing-rooms, magnificent with tapestries and inlaid furniture; the pictures by Vandyke. Then, in an awesome manner she suddenly stopped, and said in a low confidential voice, —

"The Countess herself is above stairs."

"How many feet high is the Countess? I'd give a quarter —"

Tommy's intended remark was checked by Master Lewis.

The lady requested a fee on showing the party back to the lodge and dismissed Master Lewis with a stiff bow that indicated a want of confidence in American respect for the great and mighty Guy and his successors.

CHAPTER X.

A VISIT TO OXFORD AND WOODSTOCK.

A University a Thousand Years Old. — Woodstock. — Fair Rosamond. — Old Ballad. — The Head of Brass that Spoke.

"BEAUTIFUL! beautiful!" exclaimed Wyllys Wynn, as the city of Oxford appeared in view. "It looks like a city of churches."

"It is indeed a city of institutions," said Master Lewis.

"It is a very old city, is it not?" asked Wyllys.

"It is said to have been the residence of Alfred the Great, and of King Canute. The University of Oxford was, according to tradition, founded by Alfred the Great."

"If it be so, what a monument the good king left behind him! It was this king, was it not, whose mother offered a beautiful manuscript to the one of her four sons who would first learn to repeat it from memory? Alfred, although he was a mere child and could not read, induced an instructor to teach him the manuscript, and so secured the prize."

"This was the king," said Tommy Toby, "who,

ALFRED AND HIS MOTHER.

when flying from the Danes in disguise, was left by a rustic's wife to watch some cakes that were baking by the fire."

"And let them burn," said Wyllys.

"The woman," said Tommy, "gave him a gentle hint, saying that if he was too lazy to watch them, he would be glad enough to eat them when they were cooked. I have heard my mother make very similar remarks."

CANUTE AND HIS COURTIERS.

"Canute, of whom you spoke, was the king who ordered his throne to be placed on the margin of the sea," said Wyllys to Master Lewis, "and then commanded the sea to rise no farther."

"But the sea rose," said Master Lewis, "and the king refused to wear again his golden crown for ever, resolving to serve only that King who rules the sea."

"The history of Oxford covers a period of a thousand years," continued Master Lewis. "Here Queen Matilda, or the Empress Maud, as she was called, because she had been the wife of the German Emperor, was besieged by King Stephen, who had usurped the throne, and thence she fled from him one snowy day, herself and attendants dressed in white that they might not be discovered; here the people closed the gates against William the Conqueror; here Richard I. was born, and here Ridley, Latimer, and Cranmer were burned. The early history of nearly all great English scholars for many centuries is associated with the colleges in this place."

FLIGHT OF EMPRESS MAUD.

"How green are the English meadows with their hedgerows and trees!" said Wyllys.

"And how bright are the streams that run among them! An English landscape is more rich and varied than an American."

"I never would tell of it," said Tommy. "Grass is grass, and we have just as good grass at home as anywhere."

DEATH OF LATIMER AND RIDLEY.

"We have no buildings at home that are quite equal to Warwick Castle," said Frank.

"It is better to admit excellences frankly wherever one is," said Master Lewis, "and never let any prejudice color an opinion. When one is travelling it is well never to make a comparison."

Few scenes are more charming, especially on a long sunny summer afternoon, than the college buildings of Oxford, separated by gardens, meadows, and rows of venerable trees, the latter as old as the roofs and spires that rise above them.

While at Oxford the boys were taken to Woodstock, a distance of some eight miles. The old ballad of "Fair Rosamond" so haunted the mind of Ernest Wynn, at Oxford, that he induced Master Lewis to make an excursion to Woodstock, the scene of the fancied tragedy.

"I have seen Kenilworth, the scene of one of Walter Scott's romances," said Ernest; "have been among the associations of 'Ivanhoe,' and 'Peveril of the Peak,' and I shall always be glad to have seen the place of the novelist's other English fiction."

The town of Woodstock once constituted a part of the royal demesnes. Here Ethelred held a council, and Alfred the Great translated the "Consolations of Boethius." The history of the old palace of Woodstock is associated with dark romances, splendid cavalcades, and crumbled kings and queens.

Not a vestige of the palace now remains; its site is merely marked by two sycamore trees.

The famous Rosamond's Bower, Maze, or Labyrinth seems to have consisted of a succession of under-ground chambers, and is thought to have existed before the time of King Henry II., who is supposed to have used it to hide Fair Rosamond from his jealous queen. 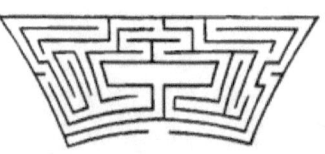 There was but one way into it, though there were many ways that would lead astray any one who should try to find the right passage. It may have been like the following diagram, which may puzzle the reader who attempts to find an open way to the centre.

Henry II. had married Eleanor of Aquitaine, a woman of bad reputation, full of craft and wickedness, whom the French king had put away. But he gave his affections to Rosamond Clifford, whose beauty had charmed him when he first met her in the valley of Wye. It is said that she supposed herself wedded to him; but however this may be, she and not Eleanor was the spouse of his heart. She pined away in the seclusion that the king provided for her, but he was true to her in her illness; he hovered around her sick bed, and at last, when she was laid away to rest in the chapel at Edstowe Nunnery, he kept her grave bright with lights and sweet with flowers. The story of her being poisoned by Queen Eleanor is a fiction, although it is said the Queen discovered her place of concealment, and administered to her a severe reproof.

A STUDIOUS MONK.

The atmosphere of learning dispels superstition, but history clings fondly to the fine old legends of the past that gather around them unreal lights and shadows. It is not strange that Oxford, the quiet valley town, hidden even to the bases of its pinnacles, spires, and towers in ancient groves, through which glide the waters of the Thames, should still preserve traditions of the wonder-working gifts of its early philosophers, whom ignorance associated with the magical arts and regarded as more than men.

It is related that two old Oxford monks made a head of brass that spoke.

AN OLD TIME STUDENT.

These wise monks discovered from their wonderful books (the like of which are not now to be found in any of the twenty colleges) that if they were able to make a head of brass that could speak, and if they could *hear* it speak within a month, they would be given the power to surround England with a magic wall of brass.

So they studied their folios, and found out the chemistry of making the wonderful head.

They listened to hear it three weeks, and then became irresistibly sleepy. So they intrusted a servant to listen, and to wake them if the statue should begin to speak.

When they were well asleep, the head said, —

"Time is."

Then it said,

"Time was."

The servant, not knowing the secret of the monks, failed to awake them as he had been ordered to do, and down came the figure with a fearful crash; and England has remained without any other wall of brass than enters into an Englishman's composition to this day.

CHAPTER XI.

LETTERS AND EXCURSIONS.

An English Skylark. — Letter from George Howe. — Tommy's Account of his Nottingham Adventure. — Glastonbury Abbey. — The Beginning of the English Church. — St. Joseph of Arimathæa and the Glastonbury Thorn. — Story of St. Dunstan and the Devil.

MASTER LEWIS set apart a day at Oxford for leisure, writing, and rest.

In the morning, after breakfast, the Class took a walk to the suburbs, and rested on some wayside seats overlooking the Thames.

It was a beautiful morning, cool and still. The world of sunlight all seemed to be above the trees, an over-sea of gold, of which the long arcades of intermingling boughs afforded but glimpses.

Near the wayside resting-place was a field bordered with trees. A speck of a bird rose from it out of the grass uttering a few notes that attracted the boys' attention. Up, up it went like a rocket, and as it rose higher and higher its song became sweeter and sweeter, — a happy, trilling melody, which made every boy leap to his feet, and try to find a place where he could see it through the openings in the trees.

"The bird seems to have gone straight up to heaven," said Wyllys Wynn. "I can hardly see it; but I can hear its melody yet."

"That is an English skylark," said Master Lewis, "so famous in pastoral poetry. You now understand Tennyson's meaning when he says, —

"'The lark becomes a sightless song.'

I am glad you have seen it. I wish we might see more of common sights and scenes.

"I have here a letter from George Howe and Leander Towle, which greatly pleases me. My object is to take you to historic scenes. George and Leander have different tastes from yours, and expect to follow different occupations. They are making their journey a study of common life and its pursuits, as I would have them do."

"Will you not read their letter to us?" asked Ernest.

"That was just what I was about to do," said Master Lewis.

CAEN, NORMANDY, July.

DEAR TEACHER: —

I begin my letter here in this city, which I suppose has an atmosphere of old history, but which is interesting to me because it is the centre of the "food-producing land" of France, as Lower Normandy is well called. All of this part of the country through which I have passed is a scene of thrift, productiveness, and plenty. The people are all busy and happy. Occupied minds are always happy, I believe.

How did we get here?

We rode a part of the way to London on what is called, I think, Parliamentary trains. This is not a train of grand coaches for the use of members of Parliament, but a sort of slow-coach train which Parliament has enacted shall carry cattle, produce, and commercial necessities for a fixed rate a mile. Or this is the way in which the running of these cheap trains was explained to me.

It would have been a hard ride, had not new scenes been continually coming into view, and the train have gone so slowly that we were enabled to enjoy them almost as well as though we had been riding on an English stage-coach. I was so interested in the new objects that presented themselves that I entirely forgot the manner of conveyance.

I shall never forget that ride: it was like viewing a long panorama.

It cost me only about £1 or $5.00, to travel from Scotland to London.

We took a lodging room in London which cost us a shilling a night apiece. While in London I visited the Tower, Westminster Abbey, Windsor, and the principal Parks. The half day spent in Westminster Abbey was worth all the discomforts of the journey across the sea.

We also made a journey to Sydenham Crystal Palace, — an immense museum of novelties, to which the admission is only one shilling. It is probably the first palace ever built for the people, and I like the idea of a people's palace better than a king's. It occupies with its grounds about three hundred acres, and cost nearly £2,000,000. Twenty-five acres of glass were used in its construction. The museum is full of the products of industry of all countries and times. Think of it — all for one shilling! It is a thing to make one always respect the English people.

I need say very little of the tombs of the twenty or thirty kings and queens in Westminster Abbey. I was first impressed with the value of fame when I read inscriptions to persons once famous of whom I never heard, — Thomas Shadwell, Poet Laureate in the Court of William III.; Mrs. Oldfield, whom we are told was buried "in a fine Brussels lace head-dress," — and I thought, Well, all men can do is to perform their duty, and time will one day make forgotten Thomas Shadwells and Mrs. Oldfields of them all.

While in London I made also a pleasant excursion into Berkshire, and there I saw the famous White-Horse Hill. It is said that the figure of the White Horse on the hill was first made by Alfred the Great a thousand years ago,

to commemorate the defeat of the Danes, — the White Horse being the standard or national emblem of the Danish chief. Whatever may have been its origin, it is *now* made by annually cutting about an acre of turf away from the chalk beneath it. This work is performed during a festival in its honor, and is called "Scouring the White Horse."

While in Berkshire I saw an odd picture, not of a castle, but of an old English gentleman's residence, which was truly castle-like in appearance, and which furnishes a happy suggestion to people who do not like to live long in any one place. It was a tun on wheels, and it had been used by an over-taxed and indignant democrat for the purpose of having no fixed locality, and so to avoid assessment.

In London I made a study of the cheapest way of getting to Paris, and of seeing the most on the journey. I found I could take a returning produce boat at Southampton for Lower Normandy at a trifling cost, and could go on a produce train from Caen to Paris as inexpensively.

We took a third-class ticket to Southampton. What a delightful ride it was! Out of the smoke of London into the blossoming country, among landscapes of cottages and gardens, — thatched cottages, cottages covered with old red tiles, cottages whose gardens seemed to climb up embankments to the roofs; past wheat fields so full of poppies that they seemed like poppy-fields in full bloom! I saw one field completely covered with red, purple, yellow, and white poppies. It was an exquisitely beautiful sight, — nothing but bright color.

The steamer we took was employed simply for the exportation of Normandy butter, potatoes, and other farm produce. It comes to England loaded, and goes back empty. I obtained passage for 10 francs, and what I saved by travel on the water I intended to make up by a longer trip by land.

We were much tossed about by the tides of the English Channel, but arrived safely at Cherbourg, and went by rail immediately to Bayeux, a dreamy, ecclesiastical city that the battles of the past seem to have left in strange silence. I spoke at the beginning of my letter of the activity and thrift of Lower Normandy, but Bayeux is the stillest city I ever saw.

FAC-SIMILE OF THE BAYEUX TAPESTRY.

Here, in the Public Library, we saw the famous Bayeux Tapestry, which is displayed under a glass case; is two hundred and fourteen feet long and contains over fifteen hundred figures. The canvas is embroidered in woollen thread of various colors, the work of Matilda and her maids. I make a copy from a sample picture of the exact size of the thread used.

One may read on this fabric the history of the Norman Conquest of England. It is the most novel work of history I ever saw.

The farming districts of Normandy seem indeed like Arcadia: farmers mean business here, and thrive by thrift. Their sons and daughters, I am told, do not run off to the city. I have never seen a people whose habits I like so well.

Give our regards to all.

GEORGE HOWE.

P. S. We are on our way to Paris, riding through a country of old churches, castles, and flowers, on a produce train.

"I think," said Master Lewis, "that George and Leander are, after all, making a very delightful tour; they certainly are getting better views of common, practical life abroad than we are. I am glad that they had the independence to make the journey in this way."

"How much do you think their whole tour will cost them?" asked Ernest.

"It will cost each of them less than either you or I have paid for a single ocean passage," said Master Lewis.

The boys spent the afternoon in letter-writing.

Tommy Toby wrote a long letter to George Howe.

"I have taken George into my confidence," said he, after tea, as Master Lewis and the boys were sitting by the open windows of the hotel, "and have given him an account of my hunting adventure in Nottingham."

"Suppose you read the letter to us," said Master Lewis.

Tommy, whose nature would not allow him to keep a secret long, however disparaging to himself, seemed pleased to accept Master Lewis's suggestion.

OXFORD, July.

At Nottingham I bought a bow and arrows, and went hunting. Like you, I wanted to see the country.

I saw it.

They are very inquisitive people around Nottingham. They seem to want to know your business before you are introduced.

A little way out of the city I came to a fine old tract of country. A gate opened into some large, hilly fields, and there was a path through the fields that seemed to lead to the wood.

I opened the gate and was going towards the wood, when I heard a voice from the road, —

"Boy!"

I looked around, and made no answer.

"Where are yer going, *yer honor?*"

"I am going hunting," said I; and I walked on very fast.

I came to a wooded hill, and the scenery all around was delightful, just like a picture. Below the hill was a long pasture, and through it ran a stream of water overhung with old trees. Under the trees were some cattle.

I was going down towards the pasture when I heard a very distressing noise, —

O-o-o-o-o!

"This is an English landscape," said I to myself. "How much more lovely it is than castles, abbeys, and tombs!" and I was trying to think of some poetry, such as Frank would have quoted, when I heard that alarming sound again, —

O-o-o-o-o!

I noticed that one of the fine animals had separated himself from the rest of the herd by the shady brook, and was coming out to meet me, looking very important. Presently he put down his head, gave the earth a scrape with his foot, and then came jumping towards me, bounding and plunging over the hillocks, like a ship on a heavy sea.

I turned right around, just as I did when I saw the bear, and I remembered that Master Lewis might not like to have me venture too far in my first hunting expedition.

I ran! didn't I run? I soon heard the same deep sound again, "nearer, clearer, deadlier than before," as the reading book says.

I had almost regained the top of the hill, when the animal bellowed almost right behind me. There was a tree close by, and I went *up*. It was just as easy for me to climb it as though it had been a ladder.

The animal bounded up the hill, and stood under the tree, pawing the earth and making the same hollow noise.

I drew my bow, and let fly an arrow at him.

"Boy, come down!"

There was a thick, fat man, with a great stomach, coming up the hill. He appeared greatly excited, and quite out of breath. He presently arrived at the foot of the tree.

"Boy, bring me that bow and arrow."

I came down the tree more scared at the man than I was at the animal. I handed him the bow, and what do you think he did with it?

He gave me a dreadful cut across my back, and said,—

"Where 'd yer come from? Take *that* and THAT, and THAT, and don't yer ever trespass on my grounds again."

I promised him I never would.

I walked just as fast as I could towards the gate, and when I came to the road I was so flustrated that I went the wrong way, and wandered about in the heat for hours before I could get rightly directed towards Nottingham.

I wish you were with us at Oxford; it seems to me the most beautiful place in all the world.

It was here we heard the skylark sing. TOMMY.

The next journey of the Club was indeed *en zigzag*.

"I have allowed you to visit," said Master Lewis to the boys, "the places to which your reading has led your curiosity, most of which places I have visited before. I now wish to take you to a ruin that I have never seen, and of which you may have never heard. It is the place where, according to tradition, Christianity was first established in Great Britain; where St. Patrick is said to have preached, and where he was buried. It is the place which poetry associates with the mission and miracles of Joseph of Arimathæa; here his staff, in the shape of the white thorn, is said to blossom every Christmas."

"Glastonbury Abbey," said Ernest Wynn. "Of course there can be no truth in the tradition of Joseph of Arimathea and the White Thorn?"

"The story of Joseph's mission to England, his burial here, and his blooming staff," said Master Lewis, "is undoubtedly a fiction, like the legend which claims that the stone in the old Scottish Coronation

Chair in Westminster Abbey is the one on which Jacob rested when he saw the vision of angels. But Glastonbury Abbey was possibly the first Church in England. Here were the monuments of King Arthur, King Edmund, and King Edgar; and even old King Coel. St. David, and St. Dunstan are said to have been buried here."

"What! the St. Dunstan that the devil tried to tempt?" asked Tommy.

"The St. Dunstan that the devil did tempt, I fear," said Master Lewis.

"I would like to hear the story of his temptations," said Tommy, "as we are going to Glastonbury."

THE STORY OF ST. DUNSTAN'S TEMPTATION.

"St. Dunstan," said Master Lewis, "was Abbot of Glastonbury Abbey, and was a very ambitious man.

"He caused a cell to be made in which he could neither stand erect nor lie down with comfort. He retired to this cell and there spent his time in working as a smith, and — so the report went — in devotion.

"Then the people said, 'How humble and penitent Dunstan is! He has the back-ache all day, and the legs-ache all night, and he suffers all for the cause of purity and truth.'

"Then Dunstan told the people that the devil came to tempt him, which, with his aches for the good cause, made his situation very trying.

"The devil, he said, wanted him to lead a life of selfish gratification, but he would not be tempted to do a thing like that; he never thought of himself. O no, good soul, not he!

"The people said that Dunstan must have become a very holy man, or the devil would not appear to him *bodily*.

"The devil came to him one day, he said, as he was at work at his forge, and, putting his nose through the window of his cell, tempted him to lead a life of pleasure. He quickly drew his pincers from the fire, and seized his tormentor by the nose, which put him in such pain that he bellowed so lustily as to shake the hills.

"The boy-king Edred, who filled the throne at this time, was in poor health, and suffered from a lingering illness for years. He felt the need of the counsel of a good man, and he said to himself, —

"'There is Dunstan, a man who has given up all selfish feelings and aspirations, a man whom even the devil cannot corrupt. I will bring him to court, and will make him my adviser.'

"Then pure-hearted Edred brought the foxy prelate to his court, and made him, of all things in the world, the royal treasurer; and he took such good care of the money entrusted to his keeping that he was speedily released from the responsibility. He seems to have been very easily tempted during his political career."

The next day the party was borne away from shady Oxford, where one would indeed like to tarry long in the midsummer days, to the old city of Bristol, famous in the Roman conquest of Britain. In the journey the gay poppy-fields and the picturesque cottage scenes, which give a charm to the English landscape, often flitted into and out of view, reminding the boys of George Howe's letter.

Glastonbury Abbey is indeed an interesting ruin. It stands apart from the popular lines of travel, and so it figures little in the narratives of those who make short tours abroad.

Think of the ruins of a church at least fourteen hundred years old! A church that Joseph of Arimathæa, who provided the tomb for Jesus, is reputed in the old monkish legends to have founded, and where St. Patrick and St. Augustine probably did preach, and where in the Middle Ages the remains of good King Arthur were disenterred!

Of the great church and its five chapels there yet remain parts of the broken wall, and the three large crypts where the early kings of England and founders of the English Church were buried. A little westward

ST. AUGUSTINE'S APPEAL TO ETHELBERT.

from the ruin stands the beautiful Chapel of St. Joseph of Arimathæa.

"I do not wonder," said Wyllys Wynn, "that the old English people liked to believe that their church sprang from the mission of so amiable a saint as St. Joseph."

"Christianity," said Master Lewis, "was really first established in Great Britain in 596 by St. Augustine and forty missionaries who came with St. Augustine from Rome to preach to the Anglo-Saxons. These missionaries were kindly received by King Ethelbert, whose wife was already a Christian. It is related that one of the Saxon priests, to see if indeed his gods would be angry, went forth on horse-back, and smote the images the people had been worshipping. To the astonishment of the Saxons no judgment followed. The king was baptized, and the missionaries baptized ten thousand converts in a single day in the river Swale. The Christian religion had been preached in Britain before, but not generally accepted."

THE SAXON PRIEST STRIKING THE IMAGES.

"I like the association of St. Joseph's name with this old ruin so well," said Wyllys, "that I wish to see the staff that you say is believed to bloom at Christmas."

On the south side of Glastonbury is Weary-all Hill. It owes its name to a very poetic legend. It is said that St. Joseph and his companions, *all* of them *weary* in one of their missionary journeys, here sat down to rest, and the Saint planted his staff into the earth, and left it there. From it, we are told, springs the famous Glastonbury Thorn which blossoms every Christmas, and whose miraculous flowers were adored in the Middle Ages. Such a shrub still remains which blooms in midwinter, and perpetuates the memory of the pretty superstition.

CHAPTER XII.

LONDON

London. — Westminster Abbey. — Westminster Hall and Parliament Houses — The Tower. — Sir Henry Wyatt and his Cat. — Madame Tussaud's Wax Works. — Tommy Accosts a Stranger. — Hampton Court Palace. — Stories of Charles I. and Cromwell. — The Duchess's Wonderful Pie. — The Boys' Day. — Tommy goes Punch and Judy Hunting. — Street Amusements. — Tommy's Misadventure. — George Howe's Cheap Tour. — Windsor Castle. — Story of Prince Albert and his Queen. — Antwerp.

THE train, from its sinuous windings among old English landscapes and thickly populated towns, seemed at last to be gliding into a new world of vanishing houses and streets.
It suddenly stopped under the glass roof of an immense station, where a regiment of porters in uniform were awaiting it, and where all outside seemed a world of cabmen.

London! — the world's great city, the nations' bazaar, — where humanity runs in no fixed channels, but ceaselessly ebbs and flows like the sea. Cabs, cabs! then a swift rattle through rattling vehicles, going in every direction, on, on, on! Names of places read in histories and story-books pass before the eye. The tides of travel everywhere seem to overflow; all is bewildering, confusing. What a map a man's mind must be to thread the innumerable streets of London!

The Class stopped at a popular hotel in a fine part of the city, called the West End. It is pleasanter and more economical to take furnished lodgings in London, if one is to remain in the city for a week or more, but as Master Lewis was to allow the boys but a few days' visit, he took them to a hotel in a quarter where the best London life could be seen.

174 ZIGZAG JOURNEYS, OR, VACATIONS IN HISTORIC LANDS.

The London cabs meet the impatient stranger's wants at once, and the boys were soon rattling in them about the city, out of the

WESTMINSTER ABBEY.

quarter of stately houses into the gay streets of trade, which seemed to them indeed like a great world's fair.

"This is Pall Mall [Pell Mell]," said Frank to Tommy, as their cab rounded a corner.

"It seems to be all *pell mell* here," said Tommy. "Had the poet been to London when he wrote, —

> "' Oh, then and there was hurrying to and fro '?

But this street has a more quiet look. What splendid houses!"

"Those," said Frank, "are the houses of the famous London Clubs."

The first visit that the boys made was to that time-honored pile of magnificence into which kings and queens for centuries have gone to be crowned and been carried to be buried, — Westminster Abbey.

The party entered at the western entrance, which commands an awesome, almost oppressive, view of the interior. In the softened light of the stained windows rose a forest of columns, rich with art and grandly gloomy with the associations of antiquity. Far, far away it stretched to the chapel of Edward the Confessor, a name that led the mind through the faded pomps of the past almost a thousand years.

Monuments of kings and queens, benefactors and poets, beginning with old Edward the Confessor and coming down to the Stuarts; of Eleanor, who sucked the poison from her husband's wounds, and Philippa, who saved the heroes of Calais. Here Bloody Mary, Queen Elizabeth, and Mary, Queen of Scots, sleep in peace in the same chapel; and here the merry monarch, Charles II., lies among the kingly tombs without a slab to mark the place.

The new, Houses of Parliament which stand between the Abbey and the Thames are the finest works of architecture that have been erected in England for centuries. They form a parallelogram nine hundred feet long and three hundred feet wide. The House of Lords and House of Commons occupy the centre of the building. Between these two halls of State rises a tower three hundred feet high. At each end of the building are lofty towers; the Victorian Tower, three hundred forty-six feet high, and a clock tower, in which the hours are struck on a bell called Big Ben, which weighs nine tons.

The entrance to the Houses of Parliament is through old Westminster Hall, ninety feet high and two hundred and ninety long, whose gothic roof of wood is the finest specimen of its kind in English art, and is regarded as one of the wonders of human achievement.

It was in this hall that Charles I. was tried for treason, and condemned; and it was here, at the trial, that the words of a mysterious lady smote Oliver Cromwell to the heart.

"The Prisoner at the bar has been brought here in the name of the People of England," said the solicitor.

"Not half the people!" exclaimed a mysterious voice in the gallery. "Oliver Cromwell is a *traitor!*"

The assembly shuddered.

"Fire upon her!" said an officer.

They did not fire. It was Lady Fairfax.

Westminster Bridge, one thousand one hundred and sixty feet long, is near the clock tower, and here the Class took its best view of the Parliament Houses.

The next day the Class visited London Tower and the relics that recall the long list of tragedies of ambitious courts and kings.

"This," said the guide, as the Class was taken into an apartment in the White Tower, an old prison whose walls are twelve feet thick, "is the beheading block that was used on Tower Hill. The Earl of Essex was beheaded on it; see the *dints!*"

An axe stood beside the block, which is kept on exhibition in one of the rooms in which Sir Walter Raleigh was confined.

"Where were the children of Edward murdered?" asked Frank Gray, after being shown the place of the execution of Anne Boleyn.

"In the Bloody Tower," said the guide. "I am not hallowed to admit visitors into that."

"We are a class in an American school. Could you not make some arrangement to admit us?" asked Wyllys.

TRIAL OF CHARLES I

The guide left the party a few minutes, and then returned with a bunch of keys.

He led the way to a small room in which the little sons of Edward had been lodged, to be accessible to the murderers. Here the unhappy children were smothered in bed. The room, apart from its dreadful associations, was a pleasant one looking out on the Thames.

The party was next shown the stairs at the foot of which the remains of the princes were discovered.

"I can imagine," said Ernest Wynn, "the life of the boys in the Tower. How they went from window to window and looked out on the Thames, the sunlight, and the sky as we do now; how they saw the bright, happy faces pass, and children in the distance at play; how they watched, it may be, the lights in their dead father's palace at night, and how they wondered why the freedom of the gay world beyond the prison was denied them. It is said that an old man who loved them used to play on some instrument in the evening under the walls of the Tower, and thus express to them his sympathy which he could not do in words."

"The burial of Richard III., who caused the death of the royal children," said Master Lewis, "was almost as pitiful as that of the princes themselves. After the fatal battle, his naked body was thrown upon a sorry steed and carried over the bridge to Leicester amid derision and scorn. For two hot summer days it was exposed to the jeers of the mob, and then was laid in a tomb costing £10 1s., to rest fifty years. The tomb was dashed in pieces during the Reformation, the bones thrown into the river, and the stone coffin, according to tradition, used as a horse-trough."

The collection of armor in an apartment of the Tower called the Horse Armory, a building over one hundred and fifty feet long, presented a spectacle that filled our visitors with wonder. It seemed like a sudden reproduction of the faded days of chivalry. On each side of the room was a row of knights in armor, in different attitudes, looking as though they were real knights under some spell of enchantment, waiting for the magic word to start them into life again.

The Jewel Tower did not so much excite the boys' astonishment. It was like a costumer's shop; and even the royal crown of England wore an almost ridiculous look, civilization and republican progress have so far outgrown these theatrical playthings. The Queen's

BURIAL OF RICHARD.

diadem, as it is called, was indeed a glitter of diamonds, and the royal sceptres of various devices carried one back to the days of Queen Esther.

"Among the stories told of the prisoners in the Tower," said Master Lewis, "there is one that is pleasant to remember. Sir Henry Wyat was confined here in a dark low cell, where he suffered from cold and hunger. A cat came to visit him at times, and used to lie in his bosom and warm him. One day the cat caught a pigeon and brought it to him to eat. The keeper heard of pussy's devotion to the prisoner, and treated him more kindly. When Wyat was released, he became noted for his fondness for cats."

Leaving the Tower, the boys stopped to look at the Traitor's Gate, which had clanged behind so many illustrious prisoners brought to the prison in the fatal barge; Cranmer, More, Anne Boleyn, bad men and good men, how it swung behind them all, and ended even hope! With sober faces the boys turned away.

The Zoölogical Gardens in Regent's Park presented the boys, on the day after their visit to the Tower, a more cheerful scene. Who that has read of the London "Zoo" has not wished to visit it? Here specimens of the whole animal kingdom may be seen, and one wanders among the immense cages, artificial ponds, bear-pits, enclosures of tropical animals, reptile dens, feeling as free and secure as Adam appears in the picture of Naming the Creation.

Here, unlike a menagerie, the animals all have room for the comforts of existence. The rhinoceroses have a pond in which to stand in the mud, and the hippopotami may sport as in their native rivers.

The British Museum, with its Roman sculptures, Elgin marbles, and almost innumerable classic antiquities, and St. Paul's with its fifty monuments of England's heroes and benefactors, presented to the Class an extended view of the world's history. Sight-seeing became almost bewildering, and when it was asked what place they next should visit, Tommy Toby replied, —

"I feel as though I had seen almost enough."

"Let us visit Madame Tussaud's wax works," said Master Lewis.

"Are they like Mrs. Jarley's 'wax figgers?'" said Tommy; "if so I would like to go. Who was Madame Tussaud?"

"She was a little French lady who took casts of faces of great men, sometimes after their death or execution, and who died herself some twenty or more years ago, at the age of ninety years."

The price of the exhibition was a shilling, and —

"For the Chamber of Horrors a sixpence hextra," said the man admitting the party. Each one paid the "hextra" sixpence.

There were three hundred figures in all, supposed to be exact representations of the persons when living. In a room called the Hall of Kings were fifty figures of kings and queens, reproducing to the life these generally condemned players on the stage of English history.

A clever, winsome old man sat on one of the benches in the place, holding a programme in his hand, and now and then raising his head, as from studying the paper, to scrutinize one or another of the astonishing works of art.

Tommy sat down beside the much interested, benevolent-looking old gentleman, and said, —

"It was not George Wilkes Booth who killed President Lincoln, it was —

"Well, if this don't cap the whole! Why, *you* are a 'figger,' too."

And so the mild, attentive-looking old gentleman proved to be.

The Chamber of Horrors revived the feeling the visitors had felt in the Tower. It was a collection of representations of criminals. Among the relics is the blade of the guillotine used during the Reign of Terror in France, which is said to have cut off two thousand heads.

Hampton Court Palace, the gift of Cardinal Wolsey to Henry VIII., and probably the most magnificent present that a prelate ever gave a king, next received our tourists' attention. The palace originally consisted of five courts, only a part of which now remain, but which assist the fancy in stereoscoping the old manorial splendor Here Wolsey lived in vice-regal pomp, and had nearly one thousand

WOLSEY SERVED BY NOBLES.

persons to do his house-keeping, and noble lords, on state occasions, waited upon him upon bended knees.

The establishment at this time contained fifteen hundred rooms.

Edward VI., the last of the boy-kings of England, a youth noted for his piety and love of learning, was born here, and here spent in scholarly occupations a part of his short life. Catharine Howard, who

WHITEHALL.

for a long time held the affections of Henry VIII., and who in his best years greatly influenced his conduct by her wisdom and accomplishments, was first acknowledged as queen here; and here also Henry married another Catharine,— Catharine Parr, his sixth and last wife. Bloody Mary kept Christmas here in 1557, when the great hall was lighted with one thousand lamps.

Our visitors found Hampton Court open to the public,— a place of rare freedom where people go out from London and enjoy the grounds much as though it were their own. It is in fact a grand picture gallery and a public garden.

"Wolsey gave this palace to the king," said Master Lewis; "and the king was sporting in the palace when he received the news of the

WOLSEY'S PALACE.

death of the Cardinal, who was stricken with a mortal sickness near Leicester Abbey, soon after having been arrested for high treason. The sad event did not seem to give the king the slightest pain. Such is the value of the presents of a corrupt friendship.

"Charles I. resided here at times. Here he brought his young bride when all London was reeking with the pestilence.

"Charles had three beautiful children, and was fond of their company. Once, it is said, when he was with them at a window of Hampton Court Palace, a gypsy appeared before him and asked for charity. He and the children laughed at her grotesque appearance, which angered her, when she took from her basket a glass and held it up to the king. He looked into it and saw his head severed from his shoulders.

"The king gave her money.

"'A dog shall die in this room,' she said, 'and then the kingdom which you will lose shall be restored to your family.'

DEATH OF CARDINAL WOLSEY.

"Many years passed; and Oliver Cromwell, attended by his faithful dog, came to Hampton Court Palace and slept in this room. When he awoke in the morning, the dog was dead.

"'The kingdom has departed from me,' he said, recalling the gypsy's prophecy; and so it proved.

"Of course the story of the gypsy's mirror is untrue, but the legend is a part of the old romance of the palace; and such poetic incidents, though false colored lights, serve to impress the facts of history more vividly on the mind.

"This legend of Charles I.," continued Master Lewis, "reminds me of a more pleasant story, which I will tell you, now that you are at the

CHILDREN OF CHARLES I.

palace where the king brought his bride when life looked so fair and promising. I will call the story —

"THE DUCHESS'S WONDERFUL PIE.

There were gala days at Paris, — wedding days. Then the new Queen of England, Henrietta Maria, who had been married amid music and rejoicings and strewings of flowers, made a journey to the sea, that she might embark for England and see her new husband to whom she had been married by proxy. There were more rejoicings when she landed at Dover.

OLIVER CROMWELL.

"It was the plague time in London, so the gala days were omitted there; but the new queen had some magnificent receptions at Burleigh-on-the-hill, the residence of the king's favorite, the Duke of Buckingham.

QUEEN HENRIETTA MARIA

"There was one reception which the duke gave to the royal bride and bridegroom that was a surprise and delight. It was a banquet; the tables were sumptuous and splendid, and on one of them was a very large pie, — as large as that is supposed to be in which the four-and-twenty black-birds of nursery-rhyme fame are said to have been concealed. The pie excited wonder, but the guests all knew that it was some

" 'Dainty dish
To set before the king.'

"The banquet passed gayly, and the time came to serve the wonderful pie. The crust was being removed, when instead of four-and-twenty blackbirds flying out, up popped a little man. He was a chipper little fellow, yet very polite, and was armed cap-à-pie.

"This was the first introduction of Jeffrey Hudson to the English king and queen. The pie had been purposely constructed to hold the little fellow, who, when the duchess made an incision in his castle of paste, shifted his situation until sufficient room was made for his appearance.

"The queen expressing herself greatly pleased with his person and manners, the duchess presented him to her.

"This dwarf became very famous in the court of the queen."

The third day in London was given to the boys as their own. They were allowed by Master Lewis to go to such places as best suited their tastes. The prudent teacher had adopted this plan before, believing that the boys needed it to teach them self-reliance.

"Where will you go to-day?" asked Frank Gray of Tommy.

"Punch-and-Judy hunting," said Tommy. "The streets of London are full of exhibitions; the queerest performances you ever saw. I have been wishing some time for a chance to see sights for myself. Will you go with me?"

"Punch-and-Judy hunting?" said Frank, contemptuously. "No; I am going to make an excursion to Cambridge."

LONDON. 195

"Remember," said Master Lewis, who had heard Tommy's remark, "that London is a wilderness of streets. You must not wander far from any principal street. Never lose sight of the cabs and omnibuses."

"I feel perfectly sure that I shall need no other help than the cabman's in finding my way back. I have taken ten shillings in my purse in case of an emergency."

"Keep your purse in your pocket wherever you find yourself," said Master Lewis. "Punch-and-Judy crowds have not the credit of being the most honest people."

Tommy found the hunting for street performances indeed alluring. Every court and alley seemed alive with the most remarkable entertainments a boy could witness.

He first met three grotesque musicians who had gathered around them an audience of admiring house-maids, dilatory market-people, and unkempt children. But the hat for contributions was passed so soon after he joined himself to the music-loving company that he at once left for another performance where the call for money might not be so pressing. A fiddler with three performing dogs, that were bedecked with hats and ruffles, quite exceeded in dramatic interest the former exhibition. But the fiddler.

STREET AMUSEMENTS.

too, had immediate need of money, and Tommy remembered Master Lewis's caution about the purse, and passed on to a public place that seemed quite alive with groups of people gathered around curious sights and entertainments.

STREET AMUSEMENTS.

The pastimes here took a scientific turn. Chief among these street showmen rose the tall head of a middle-aged gentleman — "the professor" — who administered the "galvanic grip."

"Has fast has yer cured, gentlemen, pass right along, pass right along, and give others a chance. 'Ave you han hache or a pain? I say, ave you han hache or a pain? Cure ye right hup, right hup hin a minute. I'll tell you what, it is astonishing, gentlemen, what cures science will perform."

At this point some one not schooled in the mysteries of science received a very liberal dose of the "magnetic grip," and doubled his body with an "O!" that seemed to be shot out of him, when the crowd laughed and moved on.

You pay your five or ten pence and are presented with the handles forming the terminations of the electric wire: you grasp these as tight as you can, one in either hand, while the galvanist grinds away at the machine.

When a hundred or more eyes are levelled upon you he suddenly increases the motion in a manner that leaves no doubt in your mind that that man has magnetism about him, whether he be a "professor" or not. Of course your rheumatism at once disappears: it would do the same had you fallen from the roof of a house.

Tommy had a strong inclination to be "cured" by the "professor" of galvanism," but he conscientiously recalled Master Lewis's advice about the purse.

A man with a wonderfully bedecked performing monkey was leaving the square, and, as a sort of testimony to the attraction of his exhibition, a crowd of boys and girls were following him. Tommy wished to see a performance that had evidently excited so much interest, and he allowed himself to be borne along after the man in the juvenile tide. After passing through several streets, the performer stopped in an open court, but for some reason was ordered away. Tommy found himself left almost alone in an antique-looking place, where there were in sight neither omnibuses nor cabs.

"Which is the way to Regent Street?" asked Tommy of a sad-looking little girl.

"Dunno," said Sad Eyes; "'ave ye got a penny?"

"What for?"

"For tellin' ye."

Tommy made other inquiries, but received about as definite information as at first, and each person followed the unsatisfactory answer with, "'Ave ye a penny?" as though it was worth that trifling amount to open one's mouth.

An honest-looking house-wife, without bonnet or shawl, came marching along the street with an air of friendly interest.

"Will you direct me to a street where I can find a hack?" asked Tommy.

"A what?"

"A cab."

"I guess yer lost, ar'n't ye?"

"If you will be so kind as to direct me to Regent Street or Oxford Street, or Pall Mall. I will pay you."

"'AVE YOU GOT A PENNY?"

Tommy felt in his pocket for his purse. It was *not* there.

"Give me yer hand, little boy," said the benevolent-looking dame.

The two walked on through several streets, when the woman said, —

"This street will take you to Oxford Street. 'Ave you got a penny?"

"No," said Tommy; "I have lost it."

"Oh, you blackguard — "

Tommy did not stop to hear any figurative language, but found his way to Oxford Street as quickly as possible, and took with him to the hotel so deep a sense of humiliation that he did not relate the misadventure and loss to his companions.

In the evening of the boys' "own" day, George Howe and Leander Towle arrived unexpectedly at the hotel.

"We have come," said George, "to bid you good-by."

"Why good-by?" asked Master Lewis.

"We have been abroad a fortnight," said George; "have seen the capitals of Scotland, England, and France; have rode through the heart of England and the most interesting part of Normandy, and, as our money is more than half gone, we must return. The steamer leaves to-morrow."

"How much will the whole trip cost you?" asked Wyllys.

"It will cost us each $56.00 for the ocean passage both ways, and our travelling expenses and board for the two weeks have averaged to each $2.00 per day, or $28.00. The trip will cost me, well — when I have made some purchases — say $95.00, though I have not yet spent as much as this."

"Have you obtained your return tickets?" asked Master Lewis.

"Another steamer sails in a few days," said Master Lewis; "accept my invitation to remain with us over to-morrow, and visit Windsor Castle with us. It shall add nothing to your expenses."

The boys were delighted to accept Master Lewis's generous proposal. It was arranged that the next morning the whole party should go to Windsor.

"Before we go to Windsor Castle," said Frank Gray to Master Lewis, "will you not tell us something about the place?"

"Windsor Castle," said Master Lewis, "is the finest of English palaces, and is one of the residences of the royal family. In its park, Prince Albert lies buried in the mausoleum erected by the queen. Perhaps I cannot better instruct you for the visit than by telling you the story of

PRINCE ALBERT AND HIS QUEEN.

"For seventeen years Queen Victoria has mourned for one of the best husbands and one of the wisest advisers that ever a female sovereign had.

"The marriage of Victoria and Albert was a love-match; not a very common thing in unions of princes and princesses. They were first cousins, Albert's father and Victoria's mother having been brother and sister, the children of the Duke of Coburg; but, when they became engaged, their situations were very different. Victoria was the young queen of one of the mightiest and proudest empires on earth; Albert was only the younger son of a poor and petty German prince, 'across whose dominion one might walk in half a day.'

"But their relationship and the plans of their family served to bring them together at a very early age, and they were very young when their union was first thought of. Old King Leopold of Belgium was the uncle of both of them; and it was he who first conceived the idea of their marriage. But not a word was said to either of them about it until an affection had grown up between them, and it was time for the young queen to choose a partner for her heart and throne.

VICTORIA AT THE AGE OF EIGHT.

"Albert and Victoria met for the first time when they were both seventeen years old. The young prince and his brother went to England to pay a visit to their aunt and cousin, and the young couple were brought together. Albert at that time was rather short and thick-set, but fine-looking, rosy-cheeked, natural and simple in his manners, and of a cheerful disposition. He took a great deal of interest in every thing about him, and while on his visit to England spent much time in playing on the piano with his cousin Victoria, who was then a slight, graceful, and interesting girl.

"She fell in love with him at once; but he, though he liked her, was not so quickly impressed. He wrote to his Uncle Leopold that 'our cousin is very amiable,' but had no stronger praise for her. Albert then returned to the continent, and spent some years in travel and study, writing occasionally to Victoria and she to him. Meanwhile, King William IV. died, and Victoria, in her eighteenth year, ascended the British throne.

"The young prince's next visit took place in the year after this event, and now his object was to plead for the hand and heart of the young queen. Victoria could scarcely believe her eyes when she saw him. The short, thick-set boy had grown into a tall, comely youth, with elegant manners and a strikingly handsome face. Soon after, she wrote to her Uncle Leopold. 'Albert's beauty is most striking, and he is most amiable and unaffected, — in short, very fascinating.'

"A few days after his arrival, Victoria had made up her mind;

and, sending for Lord Melbourne, the prime minister, told him that she was going to marry Prince Albert. The next day she sent for the prince; and 'in a genuine outburst of heartiness and love' she declared to him that he had gained her whole heart, and would make her very happy if he would share his life with her. He responded with warm affection, and thus they became betrothed.

"The queen not only thus 'popped the question,' but insisted that the marriage should take place at an early day. This was in the summer of 1839; and, in the early winter of 1840, the young couple were married in the royal chapel of St. James, in the midst of general rejoicing, and with great pomp and ceremony.

"Such was the beginning of a happy wedded life, which lasted for over twenty years, and during which the love of each for the other seemed to increase constantly. A little circle of children was soon formed around the royal hearthstone, and the domestic life of the palace was full of contentment and good order; and, as Victoria grew older, she learned more and more of the excellent character that Providence had given her for a husband.

"While Prince Albert assumed the direction of the family, and was the unquestioned master of it in its private life, he was wise enough to be very careful how he interfered with the queen in the performance of her public duties. He knew that, as a foreigner, the English would be very jealous of him if he took part in politics, or tried to influence Victoria in her conduct as a ruler.

"At the same time, the young queen, scarcely more than a girl, needed a guiding hand, and one that she could trust. No one could be so much trusted as her husband; and Albert gradually became her adviser on public affairs, as well as the head of her household. At first, there were many grumblings and complaints about this in England; but as the purity and good sense of the prince became better known, as it became evident that his ambition was to serve the queen and the country, these complaints for the most part ceased.

"Prince Albert devoted himself, with all his heart and mind, to the duties which he found weighing upon him as a husband and father, and as the most intimate counsellor of the monarch of a great country. He denied himself many of the innocent pleasures which lay within his reach, went but little into society, and spent his days and evenings in serious occupations and in the midst of his happy family circle.

"Among other things, he took a very deep interest in the progress of art, science, and education. 'His horses,' says a writer, 'might be seen waiting for him before the studios of artists, the museums of art and science, the institutions for benevolence or culture, but never before the doors of dissipation or mere fashion.'

"It was Prince Albert who proposed and planned the great London Exhibition of 1851, the first of the series of 'World's Fairs,' which have since been so frequently held, the latest being our own Centennial; and when it had been resolved upon, it was Prince Albert's labor and energy, more than that of any other, which made it a success.

"In his own family circle Prince Albert was always kind, gentle, and indulgent, but firm and resolute in his treatment of his children. He took a great interest in their studies, and directed their education, sometimes teaching them himself; and he bestowed an anxious and fatherly care upon the formation of their manners and habits, and a right training of their hearts and minds.

"From first to last, he was as tenderly devoted to the queen as a lover. He went with her everywhere, and his tastes and hers were entirely congenial. Of a quiet and domestic disposition, he was amply content to find his pleasures in the family circle; and Victoria took a perpetual delight in his kind and cultivated companionship.

"When Prince Albert died, in December, 1861, the queen was overwhelmed with grief; and it was many years before she so far recovered from it that she could bear to show herself in public, or to take part in any social gathering or State ceremony.

"He was placed in a tomb in the beautiful park of Windsor, where she had so often roamed with him in their early wedded life; and every year, on the sad anniversary of his death, Victoria repairs to his grave, and prays, and scatters flowers on the tomb."

Windsor Castle had its rise in early Saxon times, and was made a fortress by William the Conqueror. Froissart says that King Arthur instituted his Order of the Knights of the Round Table here. King John dwelt here during the conferences at Runnymede, when the barons drove him almost to madness by compelling him to sign away his royal claims by the acceptance of the Magna Charta.

The situation of the castle is most beautiful; it overlooks the Thames, and from its tower twelve counties may be seen. The home park of the palace contains five hundred acres, and this is connected with Windsor Great Park, which has an area of one thousand eight hundred acres.

ANGER OF KING JOHN.

The beauty of St. George's Chapel greatly excited the wonder of our tourists. Here are the tombs of Henry VIII., Charles I., Georges III. and IV., and William IV.

"Here," said Wyllys Wynn, "is the finest monument I have yet seen in England. How beautifully the light is made to fall upon it!"

The monument represented a dead princess, with a sheet thrown over the body and couch, as though she had just expired. Above it the spirit of the maiden is shown in the form of an angel ascending to heaven.

"It is the tomb of the Princess Charlotte," said Master Lewis. "She was one of the most amiable princesses that ever won the affections of the English people. Her death came like a private sorrow to every family in the kingdom, and was the occasion of the most tender public expressions of grief.

"I must tell you a story," continued Master Lewis, after standing at the tomb of George III.. "that will soften your feelings, perhaps, towards one whom, for political reasons, our own history has taught us to regard as little worthy of respect; but who had great private virtues, whatever may have been his political mistakes."

In the bright avenue of elms, called the Long Walk, which connects the home park with the Great Park of Windsor, Master Lewis told the boys the story of the lamented Princess Amelia and her unhappy father, who became insane from his loss, when she died. The pathetic story made a great impression on the minds of the party, and it was several hours before they resumed their accustomed air of gayety and enjoyment. They returned to London in the late evening twilight, and the next day the party separated. George Howe and Leander Towle remained in London until the sailing of the next steamer for America; and Master Lewis and the boys under his own care took a steamer for Antwerp.

CHAPTER XIII.

BELGIUM.

BELGIUM. — DOG-CARTS. — WATERLOO. — AIX-LA-CHAPELLE AND CHARLEMAGNE. — STORY OF CHARLEMAGNE. — GHENT AND JAMES VAN ARTEVELDE. — BRUGES. — STORY OF CHARLES THE RASH. — LONGFELLOW'S "BELFRY OF BRUGES." — FRENCH DILIGENCES. — NORMANDY. — A STORY-TELLING DRIVER. — STORY OF THE WILD GIRL OF SONGI.

"ANVERS!" By this name is Antwerp known in Belgium, of which it is the chief commercial port.

The Class stopped here only long enough to visit the Cathedral, where are to be seen two of Rubens' most celebrated pictures, the Elevation of and the Descent from the Cross. The boys climbed up to the belfry of the famous spire, whose bells make the air tremble for miles with the melody of their chimes.

It was Master Lewis's plan to travel through the lower part of Belgium and through Normandy by short journeys near the coast, but he made a détour from Antwerp to Brussels that the boys might visit the battlefield of Waterloo.

The landscape along the route to Brussels was dotted with quaint windmills, reminding one of the old pictorial histories, in which Holland is illustrated by cuts of these workshops of the air.

The boys entered the city in the morning and passed in view of the great market square and its contiguous streets.

"This city," said Frank Gray, "was the scene of the grand military ball before the Battle of Waterloo.

> "'There was a sound of revelry by night,
> And Belgium's capital had gathered then
> Her beauty and her chivalry, and —'"

"They are probably country people with produce to sell," said Wyllys. "What curious head-dresses! What odd jackets! The scene does not much remind one of Byron's poetry; but it is poetic, after all!"

"I understood that we came here to study the associations of history," said Frank, "and not dog-carts."

"I came to see what I could see," said Tommy, "and not to imagine battles in the air."

DOG-CARTS.

The unexpected street scenes and the general interest of the Class in them so offended Frank that he turned his eyes with a far-away look towards the highest gables, and passed on the rest of the way to the Hotel de l'Europe in silence.

The next morning the Class left the Place Royale, in a fine English stage-coach, in company with an agent of the English mail coaches, for Waterloo, which is about twelve miles from the city. It was a bright day, and the airy road led through the forest of Soignies, — the "Ardennes" of Byron's "Childe Harold's Pilgrimage."

"And Ardennes waves about them her green leaves,
Dewy with Nature's tear-drops, as they pass."

The battlefield of Waterloo is an open plain, graced here and there with appropriate monuments, and dignified with an imposing earth mound with the Belgian Lion on its top.

STREET SCENES IN BRUSSELS.

"Here," said Frank, "the Old Guard of France, who could die but not surrender, gave their blood for the empire."

"Here," said Wyllys, "England won her greatest battle on land —"

"At the cost of twenty thousand men, as I have read," said Tommy.

"Victor Hugo," said Master Lewis, "declares that Waterloo was not a battle; it was a change of front of the nations of the world."

The Class stopped at Brussels on their return from the most peaceful plain to take a view of the Hotel de Ville, which is one of the

est town-halls in the country. Its tower is more than three hundred
and sixty feet high, and is surmounted with a colossal statue of St.

HÔTEL DE VILLE, BRUSSELS.

Michael, which looks very small indeed from the square, but which is
really seventeen feet high. The figure turns in the wind, and is the
weather vane of the city.

"I wish you to visit Aix-la-Chapelle," said Master Lewis. "The places you have seen in England and expect to see in Normandy will, I hope, leave in your mind a clear view of English history, when you shall associate them under my direction, as I purpose to have you do. To have a view of French history you will need to learn something of the old empire of Charlemagne, of which this city was the principal

CHARLEMAGNE IN COUNCIL.

capital on this side of the Alps. Here the great king of the Franks, Roman Emperor, and virtual ruler of the world was born, had his favorite residence, and here he was buried. Here, in 1165, his tomb was opened, and his body was found seated upon a throne, crowned, the sceptre in his hand, the Gospel on his knee, and all of the insignia of imperial state about him."

Through districts of pasture lands, by cliffs that looked like castles, over clear streams and past populous villages our tourists made their way to the old city of the emperor of the West. It is situated in a valley, surrounded by heights. Its town hall was built on the ruins of the palace of Charlemagne.

The grand old cathedral has sixteen sides. In the middle of the interior, a stone with the inscription CAROLO MAGNO marks the grave of Charlemagne.

"Charlemagne, like Alfred of England," said Master Lewis, "was a patron of learning; and he instituted in his own palace a school for his sons and servants. But he was a war-making king. He conducted in

CHARLEMAGNE AT THE HEAD OF HIS ARMY.

all fifty-three expeditions in Germany, Gaul, Italy, and Greece, and made himself the ruler of the greater part of Northern and Eastern Europe. He went to Rome in 800 A.D. and received a most gracious reception from the Pope, as in all his contests he had been a faithful servant of the Church.

"On Christmas day, 800 A.D. he went into St. Peter's to attend mass. He took his place before the altar, and, as he bowed his head to pray, the Pope placed the crown of the Roman Empire upon it, and all the people shouted, 'Long live Charles Augustus, crowned of God, the great Emperor of the Romans!'

"And so the king of the Franks became the emperor of the world."

The relics which the cathedral exhibits from time to time at great public festivals are remarkable as illustrations of the influence of superstition. Among the so-called *Grandes Reliques* are the robe worn by the Virgin at the Nativity and the swaddling clothes in which the infant Saviour was wrapped. It would be almost irreverent to excite ridicule by giving a list of the articles associated with the crucifixion of Christ. Among the *Petites Reliques* are pieces of Aaron's rod that budded. Upon these pretended relics the German emperors used to take the State oath at their coronations.

The Class next visited the coronation room in the Hotel de Ville, a hall one hundred and sixty feet long, where a series of impressive frescoes presents a view of the life of Charlemagne. In this hall thirty-five German emperors and fourteen empresses had been crowned.

HOTEL DE VILLE, GHENT.

VAN ARTEVELDE AT HIS DOOR.

The Class returned to Brussels, and thence made easy journeys through a fertile and thickly settled country, towards Normandy.

Ghent, a grand old city of the commerce kings of Flanders, with its quaint town-hall and its two hundred and seventy bridges, next met the eager eyes of our tourists, who stopped here briefly on their way to Bruges.

"I never hear the name of Ghent pronounced," said Master Lewis, "without recalling the scene which history pictures of James van Artevelde standing in the door of his house, when the burghers, tired of the rule of kings and nobles, came to him for counsel, and asked him to become their leader. It was really the burghers' declaration of independence, and the making one of their number, — for James van Artevelde was a brewer, — president of the rich old city. This was on the 26th of December, 1337. It was a bold stroke for liberty in the days of tyranny, and the memory of it will ever live."

"I know but little of the history of Bruges," said Wyllys Wynn to Master Lewis, during the ride to that city. "I have heard, of course, of its belfry, and I also remember what Tommy said about it in his story of Philip the Good and the Tinker. What makes the city so famous?"

"It was once," said Master Lewis, "the greatest commercial port in the world; a hundred and fifty foreign vessels would sometimes enter its basins in a single day. Its inhabitants became very rich, and its grandees lived like princes. A French queen who visited it in its high prosperity is said to have exclaimed, 'I thought myself the only queen here, but I see a thousand about me!' Twenty ministers from foreign courts had residences within its walls. It excelled all places in the manufacture of wool; and in recognition of this fact Philip the Good instituted there the Order of the Golden Fleece.

"There is an historic character whose name is associated with Bruges in a very different way from Philip the Good, — a famous son of Philip, who was called

CHARLES THE RASH.

"His surname is a picture of his character, and it seems strange that so good a duke as Philip should have had so bad a son. To wage war, harry and burn, to be engaged always in some work of destruction, was the passion of his life. He devastated Normandy, destroying more than two hundred castles and towns. He filled the land with smoke, and colored the rivers with blood.

"He succeeded to the ducal crown of Burgundy in 1467. Being the richest prince of the times, he immediately began to make preparations for war on a gigantic scale, which should add all the neighboring territories and provinces to Burgundy. He desired to extend his personal power at any expense of blood and treasure, and he mapped out plans of conquest and dreamed dazzling dreams.

"While he was getting ready for war, Louis XI. of France invited him to a conference: he hesitated, and Louis, through his partisans, incited the citizens of Liége to revolt against him. Charles then consented to the conference, but as soon as Louis arrived, he treacherously seized him and made him his prisoner. He forced him to swear a treaty on a box which was believed to contain pieces of the true cross, and which had belonged to Charlemagne. He then compelled him to go with him to Liége, and apparently to sanction the punishment of the people for the very revolt he had incited them to make.

"He conquered Lorraine, and planned to subdue Switzerland and add it to Burgundy. He entered Switzerland, captured Grandson and hanged and drowned the garrison. The Swiss rose unitedly against such a merciless foe, and utterly defeated him. But he raised another army and again entered Switzerland, full of visions of conquest. He was again defeated.

"He came back to Burgundy, morose and gloomy. His nails and beard grew long; he looked like a wild man; the people recoiled from

CHARLES THE RASH DISCOVERED.

him, and his dark character seemed to throw a shadow around him wherever he appeared.

"Lorraine, which he had conquered, rose against him. This roused him again to action: he hired soldiers, and led the way to war. He met the rebellious Lorrainers in the plain of Nancy. Here the rash duke made his last fight. It was a snowy day, and the battle was a short one, — the soldiers of Charles flying quickly before the enemy.

"When the duke was preparing himself for the battle, the gilt lion which formed the crest of his helmet fell off.

"'It is a sign from God,' said he, smitten in conscience.

"When the battle was over his body was nowhere to be found.

"They searched for it in the snow-covered fields. At last a Roman page said he had seen the duke fall. He led the people towards a frozen pond, where were some bodies lying, stripped. A washerwoman who had joined in the search, saw the glitter of a jewel on the hand of a corpse whose face was not visible. The head was frozen in the ice. The position of the body was changed. It was Charles the Rash. He was finally buried in the church of Notre Dame, whose spire you may already see shining in the sun."

The story of Charles the Rash led the Class to visit the old church of Notre Dame soon after their arrival in the courtly old city. It had a greater charm for the boys than the ornate town-hall with its famous belfry and its many bells. In a side chapel was the tomb of the rash duke and that of his daughter, Mary of Burgundy.

"I can only think of the snowy field, and the naked body frozen in the ice," said Ernest Wynn, as he left the solemn chapel.

The belfry of Bruges, of which so much has been said and sung, is really only about three hundred feet high, but affords a grand view of the surrounding country. Its chimes play by machinery four times an hour, and are regarded the finest in Europe.

We must let Longfellow tell the charming story of his visit to the old tower: —

In the market-place of Bruges stands the belfry old and brown;
Thrice consumed and thrice rebuilded, still it watches o'er the town.

As the summer morn was breaking, on that lofty tower I stood,
And the world threw off the darkness, like the weeds of widowhood.

Thick with towns and hamlets studded, and with streams and vapors gray,
Like a shield embossed with silver, round and vast the landscape lay.

At my feet the city slumbered. From its chimneys, here and there,
Wreaths of snow-white smoke, ascending, vanished, ghost-like, into air.

Not a sound rose from the city at that early morning hour,
But I heard a heart of iron beating in the ancient tower.

From their nests beneath the rafters sang the swallows wild and high;
And the world, beneath me sleeping, seemed more distant than the sky.

Then most musical and solemn, bringing back the olden times,
With their strange, unearthly changes rang the melancholy **chimes,**

Like the psalms from some old cloister, when the nuns sing in the choir;
And the great bell tolled among them, like the chanting of a friar.

Visions of the days departed, shadowy phantoms filled my brain;
They who live in history only seemed to walk the earth again;

All the Foresters of Flanders, — mighty Baldwin Bras de Fer,
Lyderick du Bucq and Cressy Philip, Guy de Dampierre.

I beheld the pageants splendid that adorned those days of old;
Stately dames, like queens attended, knights who bore the Fleece of Gold.

Lombard and Venetian merchants with deep-laden argosies;
Ministers from twenty nations; more than royal pomp and ease.

I beheld proud Maximilian, kneeling humbly on the ground;
I beheld the gentle Mary, hunting with her hawk and hound;

And her lighted bridal-chamber, where a duke slept with the queen,
And the armed guard around them, and the sword unsheathed between.

I beheld the Flemish weavers, with Namur and Juliers bold,
Marching homeward from the bloody battle of the Spurs of Gold;

Saw the fight at Minnewater, saw the White Hoods moving west,
Saw great Artevelde victorious scale the Golden Dragon's nest.

And again a whiskered Spaniard all the land with terror smote ;
And again the wild alarum from the tocsin's throat, —

Till the bell of Ghent responded o'er lagoon and dike of sand,
"I am Roland! I am Roland! there is victory in the land!"

Then the sound of drums aroused me. The awakened city's roar
Chased the phantoms I had summoned back into their graves once more.

Hours had passed away like minutes : and, before I was aware,
Lo! the shadow of the belfry crossed the sun-illumined square.

On entering Normandy, Master Lewis engaged passages on diligences, wherever a promise of a route amid pleasant scenery offered itself. It seemed to be the boys' greatest delight to ride on the top of a diligence.

These French stage-coaches are lofty, lumbering vehicles, composed of three parts. The front division is called *coupé*, and is shaped somewhat like an old-time chariot. It holds three persons. Next is the *intérieur* or inside, holding six persons, an apartment much shunned in pleasant weather in summer time. Behind is the *rotonde* which collects "dust, dirt, and bad company." Over all is the *banquette*, a castle-like position on the top of the coupé, a seat protected by a hood, or head, and leather apron.

To secure this seat beside the "driver" was Tommy Toby's highest ambition, when about to leave a newly visited place.

In one of these rides, when Tommy and Wyllys Wynn occupied his high seat, Tommy said to the driver, —

"It seems strange to me to find such great forests in old countries like England, Belgium, and France. I fancied that great tracts of wood only existed in new lands like America, or half-civilized places. Are there wild animals in the woods here?"

The driver was a French soldier, quite advanced in life. He spoke

English well, and seemed to enjoy giving the largest **possible information** to his seat companions.

"Yes, there are some wild animals left in the forest," he said,— "of the harmless kind. *Wild people* have sometimes been found in the largest tracts of forest."

"Wild people?" asked Tommy, his curiosity greatly excited. "Did you ever see a wild man?"

"No, not myself. Did you ever hear of **Peter the** Wild Boy found in the woods in Hanover?"

"Yes," said Tommy.

"There was a wild girl **found in the French** woods, not far from **Paris,** about the same time."

"Will you not tell us the story?" **asked Tommy.**

The diligence lumbered along among the **cool forest** scenery, between the walls of green trees which now and then, like suddenly opened windows, afforded extended views; and the good-natured, well-informed driver told the **two** boys the story of

THE WILD GIRL OF SONGI.

"In the year 1731, as a nobleman was hunting **at** Songi, near the ancient and historic town of Chalons, on **the river** Champagne, in France, he discovered a couple of objects at **a distance** in the water, **at** which he fired, supposing them to be birds.

"They immediately disappeared, but arose at a point near the shore, when they were **found** to be **two** children, evidently about a dozen years of age.

"They carried to the shore some fish that they had caught, which they tore in pieces with their teeth and devoured raw, without chewing.

"After their meal, one of them found **a** rosary, probably lost by some devotee, with which she seemed highly delighted. She endeavored to conceal it from her companion, but the latter made the discovery, and, filled with rage and jealousy, inflicted a severe blow on the hand containing the treasure. The other returned the blow, striking her companion on the head with a heavy missile, and bringing her to the ground with a cry of pain.

"The sisters, for such they probably were, parted. The one most injured went towards the river and was never seen or heard of afterwards. The other hurried off towards the hamlet of Songi.

"She was a strange and frightful-looking creature. Her color was black, and her only clothing consisted of loose rags and the skins of animals. The people of Songi fled to their houses and barred their doors at the sight of her.

"She wandered about the place, greatly to the terror of the villagers, but at last some adventurers determined to set a dog on her. She awaited the attack coolly, but as soon as the monster came fairly within her reach, she dealt him such a blow on the head as laid him lifeless on the spot.

"The astonished peasants kept at a safe retreating distance, not wishing a personal encounter with such a creature. She endeavored to gain admittance to some of the houses, but the quaking occupants, who seem to have fancied that the evil one himself had made his appearance, securely fastened their doors and windows.

"She at length retired to the fields and climbed a tree, where she sat, appearing to the spectators like an omen of ill to Songi.

"The Viscount d'Epinoy was stopping at Songi at this time, and, supposing the creature to be a wild girl, offered a reward for her capture.

"The excitement in the hamlet cooling, a party was formed to secure the reward. The wild girl still remained in the tree, evidently taking repose. Thinking that she must be thirsty, a bucket of water was placed at the foot of the tree. She descended, looking cautiously around, and drank, but immediately ascended to the top of the tree, as though fearful of injury.

"She was at length allured to descend by a woman, who held out to her fish and fruit. She was seized by stout men, and taken to the seat of the viscount. One of her first acts was to devour raw some wild fowl, which she found in the kitchen.

"After public curiosity had been satisfied, the viscount sent her to a shepherd to be tamed. The latter found this no easy matter, and her wildness and animal nature were exhibited in so marked a manner that she became known as the shepherd's beast.

"She sometimes escaped. Once she was missing over night, when there came a terrible snow-storm, and the poor shepherd wandered in search of her. He discovered her at last housed just as she had been in childhood, in the branches of a tree. The wind blew and the snow drifted around her, but she was loth to return. She had learned that trouble dwells in houses, and here in the tree-top, if she was cold, she was free. I wonder if she thought of her sister in whose arms she had doubtless slept in the trees, in her childhood.

"Her agility was marvellous. She would outrun the swiftest animals, even the rabbits and hares. The Queen of Poland once took her on a hunting excursion, and much amusement she afforded to the royal party. She would discover game with the shrewdness of a bird of prey, and having outrun and captured a hare, she would bring it with great eagerness to the astonished and delighted queen.

"She was once set at the table with some people of rank, at a banquet. She seemed delighted with the bright costumes, and the wit and gay spirits of the guests. Presently she was gone. She returned at last with something very choice in her apron, and with a face beaming with happiness, she approached a fine lady, and holding up a live frog by the leg said gleefully, 'Have some?'

"She dropped the frog into the plate of the startled guest, and passing around the table, with a liberal supply of the reptiles, said, 'Have some? have some?'

"The ladies started back from such a dessert, and the poor

girl felt a pang of disappointment at the sudden rejection of the offering.

"She had gathered the frogs from a pond near at hand.

"It was a long time before she became accustomed to the habits of civilization. She died in a convent."

"What a strange history!" said Wyllys Wynn. "She must have found her life in the convent very different from that of her childhood. What was her name?"

"They called her Maria le Blanc."

CHAPTER XIV.

UPPER NORMANDY.

CALAIS. — THE BLACK PRINCE. — ÉTRETAT. — FRENCH BATHING. — LEGEND. — ROUEN. — STORY OF ST. LOUIS. — STORY OF ST. BARTHOLOMEW'S EVE.

THE Class stopped briefly at Calais, and was disappointed to find a city so famous in history situated in a barren district, and surrounded with little that is picturesque. The old walls around the town are, however, pleasant promenades, and command a view of the white cliffs of England. It was here, after a siege of eleven months, that Eustace de St. Pierre and his five companions offered themselves to Edward III. as a ransom for the city, and were saved from death by the pleading of Queen Philippa. The town was a fortress then, and looked menacingly over to England. The English proudly held possession of it for more than two hundred years, or from 1347 to 1558, when it was captured in Bloody Mary's time by the French under the Duc de Guise.

"When I am dead," said Mary in her last days, "and my body is opened, ye shall find *Calais* written on my heart."

Calais recalls the stories of valor of the chivalrous campaigns of Edward III. and his son, the Black Prince, in Normandy. At Crecy, the Black Prince, when only sixteen years of age, led the English army to victory, and slew the King of Bohemia with his own hand.

King Edward watched this battle from a windmill on a hill. The French army was many times larger than the English. The Prince during the battle found himself hard pressed, and at one point the Earl of Warwick sent to the king for assistance.

"Is my son killed?"

"No, sire," said the messenger.

"Is he wounded?"

"No, sire."

"Is he thrown to the ground?"

"No, but he is hard-pressed."

"Then," said the king, "I shall send no aid. I have set my heart upon his proving himself a brave knight, and I am resolved that the victory shall be due to his own valor."

In 1356, in another campaign in Normandy, the Black Prince won a most brilliant victory at Poitiers, and captured the French King John. The latter was a brave soldier, and fought with his battle-axe until all

CAPTURE OF KING JOHN AND HIS SON.

the nobles had forsaken him. The Black Prince made a supper for him in his tent in the evening, and waited upon him at the table with his own hands. The Black Prince and the captive king rode through London together, the former in great pomp, and the latter on a cream-colored pony by his side. All of these things read prettily in history, but one is glad that the time is past when war was the game of kings, and armies were used as their playthings.

A series of easy rides near the cool sea brought the Class to the old fishing village of Étretat, now a fashionable summer resort for French artists, and a popular bathing-place for those desiring seclusion amid the coast scenery. It is situated amid rocks which the sea has excavated into arches, aiguilles, and other fantastic recesses and caverns. Its pretty châlets and villas on the hills, its gayly-dressed summer idlers, its groups of fishermen who are to be seen in all weathers, its handsome fisher girls bronzed by the sun who lead a free life by the sea, its bathers in brilliant dresses of blue serge and bright trimmings, its bracing air and usually fine weather, make it one of the quaintest and most restful nooks in France.

There are the remains of a Norman church near the sea. It is said to occupy the spot where the people watched the great flotilla of William the Conqueror drift to St. Valery, there to take the Norman army to England.

A French watering-place is quite different from an American seaside resort. You have your board and sleeping-room in one of the hotels, but your parlors, piazzas, and places of recreation are in an elegant pleasure house, called the *Casino*. For the privileges of the Casino you pay a small sum; at Étretat it amounts to about ten dollars a month. The billiard-rooms, ball-room, and the rooms for general conversation are in the Casino.

Every one bathes in the sea at Étretat, women and children, whole families together, and most of the girls are expert swimmers. It is delightful to sit upon the *shingle*, as the pebbly beach is called, and watch the sport in the sun-bright mornings or golden and dreamy afternoons. The costumes of the bathers are so pretty that the scene seems like a ball in the sea. Bathing men are stationed here and there to render any needed assistance.

The great caverns which the sea has worn in the rocks at Étretat remind one of the ruins of immense cathedrals, and are grand indeed in the light of the full summer moon.

The place abounds with story-telling fishermen. The Class was told one story here which is worthy of a poem.

"A beautiful stream once watered the valley. Its bed may still be seen, but it now runs under ground. On the stream an industrious miller built his mill and did a thriving business. One day a woman, sick and destitute, came to him for help. He turned heartlessly away from her with abuse. The poor creature raised her withered arm, and said, —

"'To-morrow thou shalt have thy reward.'

"When the miller awoke the next morning he found his mill standing on dry ground. The river had gone down into the earth, where it still runs."

The fisher's hymn which Ernest Wynn gave the Club at its first meeting was asked for here by Master Lewis, and was procured. It is sung be-

TOWER OF JOAN OF ARC, ROUEN.

fore the departure of ships and during great storms in the fishing season, being a part of the mass for seamen, or the *messe d'équipage*.

The Class left Étretat for Rouen.

"O Rouen! Rouen! it is here I must die, and here shall be my last resting-place!" said Joan of Arc at the stake. Rouen was hardly the resting-place of the heroic peasant girl, for her ashes were thrown into the Seine. But the thought of the stranger on coming to Rouen is less associated with its history under the sea-kings of the North, the

THE MAID OF ORLEANS.

Norman dukes and the English invaders, than with the hard fate and the public memorials of the simple shepherdess, who seems to have been called from her flocks to change the destiny of France.

The Class entered Rouen after a series of short, zigzag journeys partly in coaches and partly on foot, going leisurely from town to town through roads that presented to view continuous landscapes of shining orchards, ripening gardens, and resplendent poppy-fields; stopping a

Amiens, the birthplace of Peter the Hermit, meeting here and there a ruin, and finding everywhere the connecting historical links between the present and the past.

At Amiens the Class was brought into the presence of a relic which greatly excited the boys' wonder.

"This church," said their guide, taking the Class to a side chapel of the cathedral, "contains a very rare relic.— a part of the head of John the Baptist!"

Passing into the beautiful chapel the Class was shown the shrine containing the precious treasure, which consists of the supposed frontal bone, and the upper jaw of the saint.

The *valet de place* who accompanied the Class from the hotel seemed to have no doubt of the genuineness of the relic, or of the propriety of adoring it, if indeed it were real,— and he bowed reverently before the shrine.

"A very rare relic," he said.

"Wonderful!" said Frank. "I did not know that such sacred remains were anywhere to be found as are shown us in the churches of France."

"*Quite* a rare relic," said Master Lewis, coolly. "I believe that, previous to the French Revolution, several whole heads of John the Baptist were to be seen in France."

"You do not think that a church like this would be guilty of imposture, do you?" asked Ernest Wynn.

"Not wilfully. Most of these French relics were brought from Constantinople at the time of the Crusades. They may be genuine,— the people believe them so; but, in the absence of direct historic evidence, it is probable that the Crusaders were deceived in them by others, who in their turn may have been deceived.

"You will be shown wonderful relics or shrines supposed to contain them, in nearly all the great churches of France. The French people were taught their reverence for relics by St. Louis, who sought to enrich the churches of his country with such treasures."

"Who was St. Louis?" asked Ernest.

"I am glad to have you ask the question," said Master Lewis. "His name meets you everywhere in France.

STORY OF ST. LOUIS.

"St. Louis was one of the best men that ever sat on a throne. But he was influenced by the superstitions of the times in which he lived.

"His mother was a most noble and pious woman, and he was a dutiful and affectionate son.

"It was regarded as very pious at this time for a prince to go on a crusade. St. Louis was taken sick, and he made a vow that, if he recovered, he would become a crusader. On his recovery, he appointed his mother regent, and sailed with forty thousand men for Cyprus, where he proceeded against Egypt, thinking by the conquest of that country to open a triumphant way to Palestine. He was defeated, and returned to France.

"He was a model prince among his own people. He used to spend a portion of each day in charity, and to feed an hundred or more paupers every time he went to walk. He visited his own domestics when they were sick; he founded charities, which have multiplied, and to-day cause his name to be remembered with gratitude almost everywhere in France. He made it the aim of his life to relieve suffering wherever it might be found.

"It is related of him, among a multitude of stories, that he was once accosted by a poor woman standing at the door of her cottage, who held in her hand a loaf, and said, —

"'Good king, it is of this bread that comes of thine alms that my poor, sick husband is sustained.'

"The king took the loaf and examined it.

"'It is rather hard bread,' said he; and he then visited the sick man himself and gave the case his personal sympathy.

"IT IS RATHER HARD BREAD."

"Going out on a certain Good Friday barefoot to distribute alms, he saw a leper on the other side of a dirty pond. He waded through it to the wretched man, gave him alms, then, taking his hand in his own, kissed it. The act greatly astonished his attendants, but the disease was not communicated to him.

DEATH OF ST. LOUIS.

"In 1270 he started on a new crusade, but died in Tunis of the pestilence. Visions of the conquest of the Holy City seemed to fill his mind to the last. He was heard to exclaim on his death-bed in his tent, 'Jerusalem! Jerusalem! We will go up to Jerusalem!'"

One of the first places which the Class sought out in Rouen was the statue of Joan of Arc. It is placed on a street fountain near the spot where the unfortunate maid was burned. It disappointed our tourists, and seemed an unworthy tribute to such an heroic character. The great tower, called the Tower of Joan of Arc, seemed a more fitting reminder of her achievements.

The streets of Rouen are narrow, but are full of life. Rouen has been called a New Paris, and Napoleon said that Hâvre, Rouen, and Paris were one city of which the river Seine was the highway. The gable-faced, timber-fronted mansions are interspersed with evidences of modern thrift, and the Rouen of romance seems everywhere disappearing in the Rouen of trade.

The Cathedral of Rouen is a confusing pile of art; it has beautiful rose windows, and its spire is four hundred and thirty-six feet high. The old church of St. Ouen, which is larger and more splendid than the cathedral, is regarded as one of the most perfect specimens of Gothic art in the world. It is 443 feet long.

The Palais de Justice, as the old province house

INTERIOR OF ST. OUEN

or parliament house is called, is an odd but picturesque structure. It lines three sides of a public square.

PALAIS DE JUSTICE, ROUEN.

"To-morrow," said Master Lewis, after a day of sight-seeing in Rouen, "we go to the most beautiful city in all the world."

"I wish I knew more about the history of Paris," said Ernest Wynn, "now that it is so near to us. I think of it as a place of gayety and splendor, the scene of St. Bartholomew's Massacre, of the Revolution, and the Commune. It was the city that Napoleon seemed to love more than any thing else in the world. What is its early history?"

"You will read in Julius Cæsar's Commentaries, in your course in Latin," said Master Lewis, " a brief account of Lutetia, the chief town of the Parisii, a Gallic tribe that the Romans conquered. This, I think, is the oldest historical allusion to Paris, as Lutetia came to be called. It was probably an old town at the time of the Roman invasion; it was chosen by Clovis as the seat of his empire in the sixth century; it began to grow when the Northmen came sailing up the Seine in their strange ships to its gates, and made it their prey. In the tenth century it became the residence of Hugh Capet, the founder of the Capetian line of kings, and soon after increased so rapidly that it doubled in size and population. Under Henri of Navarre, in 1589, the city began to be famous for its tendencies to gayety and splendor. Louis the Great

NORTHMEN ON AN EXPEDITION.

lavished the wealth of France upon it, converting the old ramparts into picturesque public walks or boulevards, and enlarging and adorning its palaces so that they rivalled the royal structures of the East. Then Napoleon I. enriched it with the spoils of Europe, spending on it more than £4,000,000 in twelve years. Napoleon III. completed the work of his predecessors by introducing into the city all modern improvements, and making Paris in every respect the most magnificent capital in Europe.

"I have given you in the story of Charlemagne and in the visit to Aix-la-Chapelle a view of the early French Empire; in the story of St. Louis you have had a glance at France at the time of the Crusades; I think I will here tell you a story which will present to you another period of the nation's history.

THE BARQUES OF THE NORTHMEN BEFORE PARIS.

STORY OF CHARLES IX. AND ST. BARTHOLOMEW'S EVE.

"Charles IX., the twelfth king of the family of Valois, came to the French throne when only ten years of age, under the regency of his mother, that terrible woman, Catharine de Medici. He was an impulsive youth, restless and vacillating, and was left wholly to the evil influences of his mother. The first years of his reign were disturbed by the struggles between the Protestant and Catholic parties in France. These difficulties were apparently settled in 1569.

"The queen-mother, who was a Catholic, seemed to entertain kind feelings towards the Protestant leaders. The Protestant King of Navarre was promised the hand of the king's sister Marguerite, and marked courtesy and apparent kindness of feeling were shown by the royal household to many of the leading men of the great Protestant party. The latter were thus rendered unsuspicious of danger, and became almost wholly disarmed.

CATHARINE DE MEDICI.

"But Catharine de Medici, full of craft and wickedness, had resolved to destroy the Protestant power. She was fully versed in crime, and the passion for dark deeds grew upon her with years. One day she went to the boy-king, Charles, and disclosed a plot for the massacre of the Protestants of France. He listened with a feeling of horror. He had learned to love the Protestant statesmen, and to call their great leader, Coligny, 'father.' His young heart recoiled from such a deed. But his mother gave him no rest. She confided her plot to the Catholic leaders, who joined hand in hand with her to accomplish the crime. Church and State united to persuade the young king that the stability of the throne, the glory of his family, and the advancement of religious truth demanded the slaughter of the Huguenots, as the Protestant party were called. Still he hesitated; but after a little while exhibited his characteristic weakness under the influence of persuasion, and the conspirators knew his final assent was certain.

" St. Bartholomew's Day was at hand, the time appointed by the Catholic leaders, the Guises, for the work of death. Paris was full of Huguenots from the principal provincial cities, who had been drawn hither by the magnificent wedding of the Protestant King of Navarre. The preparations for the massacre were nearly complete, but the young king still hesitated to issue the fatal order.

" His mother now used every art in her power to make him place himself boldly with the Guises. As he was king, she wished the sanction of a royal edict to do her bloody work. With this the preparations for the destruction of the Huguenots would be complete. Her appeals at length so wrought upon his mind that he excitedly exclaimed, ' Well, then, kill them! kill them all, that not a single Huguenot may live to reproach me!' This frantic remark was construed as an order.

" The massacre was appointed to begin on St. Bartholomew's Eve, at the tolling of a bell. The young king was fearfully nervous and agitated during the preceding day. Just before the fatal hour, his conscience had so affected his better feelings, that he despatched orders to the Duc de Guise, countermanding the slaughter. The duke received the message as he was in the act of mounting his horse to lead the assassins.

" ' Il est trop tard !' ' It is too late !' said the duke to the bearer, and at once rode away.

" It was a still night, August 24, 1572. The defenceless Hugue-

COLIGNY.

nots were unsuspicious of danger, while armed assassins were lurking in every house. At last the heavy clang of a great bell fell on the breathless evening air, and the slaughter began.

"All that summer night the streets ran with blood. The young and the old, the daughter, the mother, the nobleman and the beggar, — all who bore the name of Huguenot, — were cut off without mercy. None were spared. Even women murdered women, and children, it is said, impelled by the maddening example, applied the dagger to other children in their beds. The streets of Paris ran with blood. From thirty to seventy thousand persons were slain in the city and in the towns of France on this night and a few days following it.

"The new Queen of Navarre, Marguerite de Valois, had gone to bed on the fatal eve, by the express order of Catharine. Just as she was going to sleep, she says, a man knocked with hands and feet at her door, shouting 'Navarre! Navarre!' The nurse, thinking it was the king, opened the door. A Protestant gentleman, bleeding, and pursued by four archers, threw himself on her bed for protection. The archers rushed after him, but were stayed by the appearance of the captain of the guard. The young queen hid the wounded Huguenot in one of her closets, and cared for him until he was able to escape. Such scenes took place in nearly all the houses of the nobility.

"Coligny was rudely murdered, and his body thrown out of the window of his apartments into the courtyard, where it is said to have been kicked by the Duc de Guise. The young king was in a court of the palace of the Louvre, with his mother, when the great bell began to toll. At first he trembled with fear and horror. He recovered presently from his fear, and, running to the palace window, became so excited at the sight of blood that he fired upon the wretched fugitives who were attempting to escape by swimming across the Seine.

"But the young king never knew a happy hour after that dreadful night. He grew pale and thin, and his tortured conscience and shattered brain called up in his solitary hours the images of the slain.

Two years after the massacre of St. Bartholomew's Eve the young king lay dying. His disease, it has been said, was caused by poison, which had been applied to the leaves of one of his favorite books for the purpose, by his unnatural mother. His sufferings were dreadful in the extreme. Historians tell us that he sweat drops of blood. His mental anguish was as fearful as his bodily distress. He would cry out to his nurse, '*Ah, nourrice, ma mie, ma bonne! que du sang, que d'assassinats! Oh quels mauvais conseils j'ai suivis! Oh Seigneur Dieu, pardonnez moi, et faites moi misericorde!'* 'Ah, nurse, my good nurse! What blood! What murders! Oh what bad counsels I followed! Lord God, pardon me! Have mercy on me!'

"Historians cover the memory of Charles IX. with infamy, but his first impulses were usually kind, and his first intentions good. He does not seem to have inherited the disposition of that monster of wickedness, his mother. His most evil acts could hardly be called his own. Left to himself he would have been deemed a most polished and amiable prince, though wanting in decision. As a victim of bad counsellors, pity should mingle with the censure that follows his name."

CHARLES IX. AND CATHARINE DE MEDICI

CHAPTER XV.

PARIS.

aris the Beautiful. — Notre Dame. — Tuileries and Louvre. — Garden of the Tuileries. — Bois de Boulogne. — Church of the Invalides. — Napoleon's Tomb. — Place de la Concorde. — Story of the Man of the Iron Mask. — Versailles and the Trianons. — Story of the Dauphin. — Fontainebleau. — The Seine. — Water Omnibusses. — A Wonderful Boat. — Tommy's French. — A Surprise. — St. Eustache. Molière. — Young French Heroes. —Wyllys Wynn's Poem.

PARIS the beautiful!
City of light hearts, smiling faces, charming courtesies, and gay scenes everywhere!
City of dark tragedies of history that have hardly left behind a scar! The tropical forest gives no warning of poison lurking under the flowers; the bright Southern sky wears no trace of the tempest. Paris says to the stranger, "I am beautiful: I have ever been beautiful, and I wear loveliness like a crown."

The streets are as gay as the summer sunshine in them; the boulevards, as the wide streets and avenues for pleasure walks are called, em channels of happiness, through which the tides of life run as lightly as they glimmer along the Seine. "La belle Paris!" says the ranger as he comes, and "La belle Paris!" he utters respectfully as he goes.

We do not wonder that the French love it; that Napoleon gloried in it, and that Mary Queen of Scots left it with a heavy heart. Here human nature has light, warmth, and glow; and love, sympathy, and patriotism are everywhere to be seen.

"Where are the ruins caused by the siege and the Commune?" asked Frank Gray, after the Class had been driven through a number of streets. "I do not see the first sign of there having been a recent war and revolution."

"In the fall of 1870, said Master Lewis, "shot and shell for a long period fell around the city and into it like rain. In the following spring the Commune was declared the government of Paris, and it seemed bent on destroying the city's beauty, and overturning its monuments of art. The Vendôme Column, which celebrated the victories of Napoleon the Great, was pulled down as a monument of tyranny; the Palace of the Tuileries and the Hotel de Ville were set on fire and the wealthy citizens who had endured the siege by a foreign foe fled from their own countrymen. To-day most of the houses destroyed by the war and the Commune are rebuilt, and the streets are as splendid as in the gay days of the Empire."

The Class took rooms in the *Grand Hotel*, one of the largest and finest houses for public entertainment in Europe. Its first visit was to the ancient Cathedral of Notre Dame, whose history is as old as Christianity in France, and which even before that period was a Pagan temple. Here *Te Deums* for all of the nation's victories have been sung; funeral orations of kings have been pronounced, confessions of sin for a thousand years have been made, and masses innumerable celebrated. Here Napoléon the Great was crowned, and Napoleon III was married. Here the Goddess of Reason, after being borne through the streets in state, was enthroned during the Revolution of 1793. It has thirty-seven chapels.

In entering the cathedral the Class seemed to be in a new world. The rose-colored windows flooded the edifice with a soft light; and beyond it was a blaze of candles amid clouds of incense, for the priests in their gorgeous vestments were administering at the altar.

The boys passed through the waves of light reverently, and stood near the altar. A choir of altar boys suddenly rose amid the smoke and lights and glitter of priestly robes, and sang most melodiously. It seemed very solemn and grand, but the thought of the associations of

THE GODDESS OF REASON CARRIED THROUGH THE STREETS OF PARIS.

the place was even more awe-inspiring. The scene was one that had been enacted for more than a thousand years, under the groined roof of the same stately edifice, and the past seemed to hang, a weight of gloom, in the very air.

On each one's paying half a franc, the Class was admitted into the sacristy, where the sacred relics, purchased in the East by St. Louis himself, are kept. Among them is a supposed piece of the true cross and a pretended part of the Crown of Thorns which was put upon the Saviour's head before the Crucifixion.

The second day that the Class spent in Paris was the most delightful of the whole tour.

"I shall go with you to-day," said Master Lewis, "to the most beautiful place in Europe, the most beautiful garden in Europe, and one of the most beautiful picture-galleries in the world."

"The Tuileries?" asked Frank.

"The Louvre?" asked Ernest.

"Both," said Master Lewis.

"The Tuileries and the Louvre are now one. Francis I. began the building of the Louvre in 1541; Catharine de Medici commenced the Tuileries in 1564; Napoleon III. united the two palaces in the four years following 1852. The two palaces have been growing about three hundred years. The Tuileries was partly burned by the Commune. The united palaces cover twenty-four acres. Think of it! Twenty-four acres of art, ornament, pictures, and splendor!"

The garden of the Tuileries is the favorite promenade of wealthy and fashionable Parisians, and seemed to the boys too beautiful for reality. Graceful statues rise on every hand from flower-beds, bowers, by cool fountains, and in the shade of grand old trees, — statues in marble, stone, and bronze; Grecian, Roman, French. Airy terraces, basins bordered with rich foliage and gorgeous flowers carry the eye hither and thither, and call out some new expression of admiration at almost every step.

"How happy the life of a French king must have been!" said Tommy Toby.

"How unhappy the lives of French kings have been!" said Master Lewis. "If you would have a view of royalty that makes a peasant's life seem desirable, read the history of the old French kings."

The beautiful forests of France extend to the very outskirts of the city. One of these, the Bois de Boulogne, is the favorite park of Paris. It contains more than two thousand acres. It has an immense aquarium, pavilions of birds, and a garden for ostriches and cassowaries, and its principal avenue is one hundred yards wide.

The Class visited this park on a beautiful afternoon, passing through the Champs Elysées, a splendid avenue filled with equipages. In this walk the boys saw the famous *Arc de Triomphe* and the *Palais de l'Industrie*, in which the World's Fair was held in 1855, when nearly two million strangers beheld Paris in her glory. The Arc de Triomphe was begun in 1806, the year of the battle of Austerlitz, and was finished by Louis Philippe. It commemorates the victories of Napoleon, and is the most magnificent imperial monument in the world.

No scene in Paris seemed to inspire a part of the Class with so much awe as the tomb of Napoleon. At the entrance to the crypt of the dome of the church of the Invalides, containing the conqueror's remains, are these words: "I desire that my ashes may rest on the banks of the Seine, in the midst of the French people whom I have loved so well."

From a balustrade above the tomb under the beautiful dome the boys looked down in silence on the sarcophagus, or stone coffin, which is of Finland granite. The monolith on which it rests is porphyry, and weighs 130,000 pounds. The monument cost nine million francs.

A beautifully tinted light fell upon the sarcophagus.

"Look," said Tommy, "see —"

An armed guard approached, with a solemn gesture of the hand. He simply said, —

"Be reverent."

GARDEN OF THE TUILERIES.

The Hotel des Invalides, an asylum for disabled soldiers, of which the church and dome are a part, was founded by Louis XIV. The dome is gilded, and is three hundred and thirty feet high.

FOUNTAIN IN THE CHAMPS ELYSÉES.

Ernest Wynn, who seemed to have a part of some old ballad always upon his lips, repeated some fine lines to Master Lewis as they went out of the church, — a quotation from an old song, entitled "Napoleon's Grave." (At St. Helena.)

> "Though nations may combat and war's thunders rattle.
> No more on thy steed wilt thou sweep o'er the plain ;
> Thou sleep'st thy last sleep, thou hast fought thy last battle.
> No sound can awake thee to glory again."

PLACE DE LA CONCORDE.

Here stood the guillotine, or rather the guillotines, on which Louis XIV. and Marie Antoinette and nearly three thousand persons perished. Here revolutionists cut off the heads of the royal family, and the people the heads of the revolutionists.

ENTRANCE TO THE LOUVRE.

Two beautiful fountains were playing on the afternoon when the Class made their visit. The sky was all rose and gold; the Seine flowed calmly along; the aspect of every thing seemed as foreign to any past association of war, tragedy, and pangs of human suffering as the figures of the Tritons and Nereids that were spouting water from the fishes in their hands.

FOUNTAIN. PLACE DE LA CONCORDE.

Leaving the Place de la Concorde, which Master Lewis said he 'elieved was constructed in part of stones of the old Bastile, the Class ent to the public square where the Bastile had stood.

"The Place of the Bastile," said Master Lewis, "now adorned by the Column of Liberty, is the site of the old Castle of Paris, which was built as a defence against the English. The castle became a prison for people who offended the French kings. The Man of the Iron Mask was confined here. It was regarded as an obstacle to liberty, and it was stormed by the people during the Revolution, and destroyed."

"Who was the Man of the Iron Mask?" asked Tommy Toby.

"That is a question that used to be asked by all the statesmen of Europe, and that has been repeated and always will be by every reader of history. It has been answered in many different ways. Books, pamphlets, and essays have been written upon the subject. It is still a secret, and seems destined always to remain so. I will give you briefly the strange history of this State prisoner."

THE MAN OF THE IRON MASK.

"During the reign of that voluptuous old monarch, Louis XIV. of France, there appeared on one of the Marguerite Islands, in the Mediterranean, a prisoner of State closely guarded, and entrusted to the especial care of a French governmental officer, De Saint Mars.

"Although confined in this obscure spot in the sea, where but little was seen or heard save a distant sail and the dashing of waters, he became a marked man among the few who chanced to meet him, and the circumstance of his concealment was in danger of being noised abroad. He was consequently removed to Paris, and immured in the cells of the Bastile.

"From the time that he began to attract attention on the island in the Mediterranean to the close of his protracted life, no one but his appointed attendants is known to have seen his face.

"His head was enveloped in a black-velvet mask, confined by springs of steel, and so arranged that he could not reveal his features without immediate detection.

"His guardian, De Saint Mars, had been instructed by a royal order, or by an order from certain of the king's favorites, to take his life immediately, should he attempt to reveal his identity.

"During his confinement on the Marguerite island, De Saint Mars ate and slept in the same room with him, and was always provided with weapons with which to despatch him, should he attempt to discover the secret of his history. If report is true, De Saint Mars might well exercise caution, for it is asserted that he was to forfeit his own life if by any want of watchfulness he allowed the prisoner to reveal his identity.

"The prisoner himself seemed anxious to make the forbidden discovery. He once wrote a word on some linen, and succeeded in communicating what he wished to an individual not in the secret of the mystery. But the *ruse* was discovered, and the person that received the linen died suddenly, being taken off, it was supposed, by poison. He once engraved something, probably his name, on a piece of silver plate. The person to whom it was conveyed was detected in his knowledge of the secret, and soon after died, as suddenly and mysteriously as the one who had received the linen.

"These incidents indicate that the prisoner was a man of shrewdness and learning.

"He was attended, during his imprisonment in the Bastile, by the governor of the fortress, who alone administered to his wants; and when he attended mass he was always followed by a detachment of invalides (French soldiers), who were instructed to fire upon him in case he should speak or attempt to uncover his face.

"These circumstances, and many others of like character, show that he was a person of very eminent rank, and that those who thus shut him out from mankind were conscious that they were committing a crime of no ordinary magnitude.

"Who, then, was this person of mystery, familiarly known as the Man of the Iron Mask?

"He is supposed by many to have been a son of Anne of Austria and the Duke of Buckingham, and consequently a half-brother of Louis XIV., and a co-heir to the throne of France. If so, it would appear that while Louis XIV. was luxuriating amid the splendors of the palace of Versailles, his brother was suffering the miseries of exile, or languishing in a dungeon, shut out not only from the outward world, but from all intercourse with mankind. But other writers think him to have been some less remarkable person.

"The iron mask, of which frequent mention has been made in sensational books, was a very simple contrivance of velvet and springs of steel."

The Class made two excursions from Paris, one to Versailles and the other to Fontainebleau.

Versailles, a town of 30,000 inhabitants, which has grown up around one of the finest palaces and parks of Europe, was originally the hunting-lodge of Louis XIII. Louis XIV. chose the place for a palace and employed almost an army of men for eleven years upon the structure. He spent upon this palace nearly £40,000,000 sterling. Thither in 1680 he removed his gay court, and here he passed in gloomy grandeur his melancholy old age.

It is a place of beautiful gardens, wonderful fountains, fine statues and walks associated with the history of kings, queens, statesmen, and scholars. The palace to the visitor seems a vast picture gallery wherein is shown the conquests of France. It is a long journey through the glittering rooms. Here you see the representation of a king in his moment of triumph, adored as a god, and there you see the same king overthrown or stretched upon his bed of death. The fountains murmur, the orange trees fill the air with perfume, and you turn from the exhibition of the glowing and faded pomps of history to the gardens, feeling that after all man's only nobility and kinship and hope of a crown lies in his soul, and it is virtue alone that makes one royal.

Two small palaces or villas in the Park of Versailles, called Great Trianon and Little Trianon, recalled to Master Lewis the happy days of the life of Marie Antoinette, which she spent here while the unseen cloud of the Revolution was gathering, and the calm settled down on Paris before the storm.

VERSAILLES.

"We have seen the places where Louis XVI. and Marie Antoinette lived and were beheaded. What became of their children?" asked Frank Gray?

"The oldest son of Louis XVI. died at the beginning of the Revolution. As it may give you a picture of the stormy times of the period, let me tell you

THE STORY OF THE DAUPHIN

"He was born at Versailles in 1785. He was a most affectionate child, and was ardently attached to his mother. He used to sport about the gardens of the palace; the very place where we are now was his play-ground.

"He would sometimes rise early in the morning to gather flowers from the gardens to lay on his mother's pillow.

"'Ah!' he would say, when weary of play, 'I have not earned the first kiss from mother to-day.'

LITTLE TRIANON.

THE DAUPHIN WITH THE ROYAL FAMILY IN THE ASSEMBLY

"The Revolution came and cast a shadow over Versailles, with all its glory. The royal family was surrounded with enemies, and was in constant terror, and the little dauphin was made unhappy by the sight of his mother's tears.

"One day a serving-woman told him that if he would procure some favor for her she would be happy as a queen.

"'As happy as a queen!' he answered: 'I know of one queen who does nothing but weep.'

"The Revolutionists overthrew the Bastile and the throne, and the members of the royal family were obliged to seek protection in the National Assembly. They were then confined in an old French prison, called the Temple.

"The king was tried by the Assembly, was condemned and executed. He deeply loved the dauphin, and parted from him with bitter grief.

"After the king's death the dauphin was the principal solace of the queen in her imprisonment. He was at last removed from the queen's apartment by an order of the Committee of Public Safety. It is related that when the guards came to take him away, his mother fought for him until her strength was exhausted, and she fell senseless upon the floor.

"After the execution of his mother he was given over to the care of a brutal shoemaker, named Simon, who endeavored to cause his death without committing palpable murder. He was ill-fed, beaten and abused, and received the name of the 'She-wolf's Whelp,' referring to Marie Antoinette.

"At this period the police were in the habit of distributing in the streets songs against 'Madame Veto,' as the queen had been called. One of the most infamous of these, as vulgar as it was brutal, had been preserved by Simon.

"One day, for the want of a new torture for the child, Simon resolved to make him sing this obscene song against his mother.

"'Come along, Capet,' said he, 'here is a new song which you must sing to me.'

"He handed the song to the dauphin. The boy saw its meaning, and with all the instincts of a susceptible nature he recoiled from the thought of reviling his mother. He laid it down on the table without saying a word.

"Simon arose in wrath.

"'I thought I said you must sing.'

"'I never will sing such a song.'

"'I declare to you that I will kill you if you refuse to obey me.'

"'Never!'

"Simon caught up an andiron, and threw it at the child with a force that would have proved fatal had he not missed his aim. His passion then gradually subsided, but the boy refused to sing.

"One day, after a system of abuses too shocking to relate, Simon seized the dauphin by the ear, and drawing him to the middle of the apartment, said, —

"'Capet, if the Vendéans were to set you at liberty, what would you do to me?'

"'I would forgive you,' replied the noble boy.

"His situation at last became wretched in the extreme. He was placed in a filthy cell where he could neither receive pure air nor have exercise; his food was scanty, his bed was not made for six months and his clothes were not changed for a year. He became covered with vermin, and the mice used to nibble at his feet. He passed the days in utter silence, wishing only to die. Once, when he had attempted to pray kneeling, he had been discovered and terribly punished, and he felt that it was not safe for him to speak even to his God.

"After the overthrow of the Revolutionary government under Robespierre, he was assigned to more merciful keepers. But his body and mind were in ruins, and all efforts to restore him proved in vain.

"It was a lovely June day in the summer of 1795. He was dying without, the air was full of sunshine, of birds and roses.

"'Are you in pain?' asked his attendant.

"'Yes,' he said; 'but not in so much as I was, the music is so sweet.'

"He presently added: 'Do you not hear the music?'

"'From whence does it come?'

"'From above.'

"His eyes became luminous; he seemed happy and peaceful, and he fancied that among the voices that seemed to be singing around him he could distinguish that of his mother. It may have been all but a dream or fancy, but it grew out of the filial devotion of his heart."

FOREST OF FONTAINEBLEAU.

Fontainebleau is one of the most ancient palaces of France; it is a labyrinth of galleries, salons, amphitheatres, secret chambers, and fantastic balconies. To traverse the palace is a journey. Like all the old

French palaces, it is surrounded with gardens, parks, and has its wood or forest. Indeed, the town of Fontainebleau is situated in a forest, which covers an extent of sixty-four miles.

IN THE WOOD AT FONTAINEBLEAU.

"Artists, poets, romancers, and lovers," says a writer, "have from time immemorial made the forest of Fontainebleau the empire of their dreams. You ought to see it in the morning when the bird sings, when the sun shines, . . . when all these stones, heaped beneath those aged trees, take a thousand fantastic forms, and give to it the appearance of the plain on which the Titans fought against Heaven. Oh, what terrible and touching histories, stories of hunting and of love, of treason and vengeance, this forest has covered with its shadow!"

St. Louis loved this forest, and Napoleon signed his abdication at Fontainebleau.

Master Lewis had allowed the boys to have a day to themselves in each of the principal places where they had stopped. If one of them wished to make an excursion on that day to some neighboring place, the good teacher made some careful arrangement for that one to do so. He was very careful about all matters of this kind, without really seeming to distrust the boys' judgment in their efforts to look out for themselves. A coach-driver, a traveller, a valet-de-place, or some person was usually employed to have an eye on the member of the Class who was allowed to make a tour to a strange place alone.

The boys, with the exception of Tommy Toby, were given a day to go where they liked in Paris. Master Lewis did not dare to allow Tommy this privilege, after his misadventure in England.

The Wynns visited the Palace of the Institute; Frank Gray, the Grand Opera House.

"I would like to go to the river this morning," said Tommy, "and sail on the —— queer boats there."

"The flies, or water-omnibuses?" said Master Lewis. "I will go with you."

Tommy looked surprised and hardly seemed pleased, not that he did not generally like Master Lewis's company, but because it looked to him like a restraint upon his freedom.

But the good teacher took his hat and cane, and Tommy did not express any displeasure in words. The two went to a splendid stone bridge called the Pont d'Jena, over the Seine.

Compared with the Mississippi, the Ohio, or the St. Lawrence, the

Seine is but a small stream. The river is lined with solid stone-work on each side, and its banks are shaded with trees. It is filled with queer crafts, and a multitude of families live on the barges that convey wood, coal, and certain kinds of merchandise from place to place.

As Master Lewis and Tommy were standing on the bridge, watching the sloops as they lowered their masts to pass under, an astonishing sight met Tommy's eyes.

It was a great boat, like a steamer, but without screw or paddles, swiftly passing up the river by means of a chain which rose out of the water at the bows, ran along the deck, turned around wheels which seemed to be worked by an engine, and then slipped overboard at the stern.

"How far can that boat go on in that way?" asked Tommy.

"The chain by which the boat is carried forward," said Master Lewis, "is *one hundred miles long*."

Master Lewis and Tommy passed some hours among the queer crafts on the river, taking passages here and there on the flies or water-omnibuses.

"Were you afraid to trust me alone this morning?" asked Tommy, on their return.

"Well, yes."

"Did you think I could not speak French well enough to go out alone?"

"Your French might not be very well understood here."

"I think I can talk simple French, such as servants could understand very well."

In the afternoon, being somewhat alone, Tommy thought he would explore the hotel, which was something of a town in itself. He descended from his apartment on the third floor, with the intention of going to the courtyard. But he could not find the place which had so attracted him from his window. He tried to go back, but lost the way even to his apartment. He descended again, but failed to find any place he remembered to have seen before. It was all as grand as a palace, but as puzzling as a labyrinth he had seen in the grounds of Hampton Court Palace.

He said to one after another of the very polite people he chanced to meet, —

"Please, sir [or madam], do you speak English?"

He received only smiles of good-will, and courteous shakes of the head, in answer to all inquiries.

Tommy remembered his French lessons. Happy thought! He accosted a servant, whose knowledge of the language he fancied might be as simple as his own: —

"*Pardon, Monsieur, voulez-vous avez la bonté de m'indiquer un valet-de-place?*"

"*Je ne comprends pas,*" said he.

"*Je ne comprends pas,*" said Tommy. "*Je ne puis pas trouver ma chambre,*" pointing upward. "*Voulez-vous m'indiquer quelqu'un qui parle l'Anglais?*"

"*Je ne comprends pas.*"

"*Ne comprenez-vous Français?*" said Tommy.

The man's face wore a willing, but very puzzled expression.

Just then a girl with a happy face came out of one of the rooms.

"Do you speak" ——

"Why, yes, of course I speak. I am very glad to meet you here. How pleasant!"

"JE NE COMPRENDS PAS."

It was Agnes, the young lady who had made herself so agreeable on the steamer.

The next morning, after a chat with Agnes, Master Lewis said to Tommy, —

"I think I will let you take a day to go where you like."

"Will you not let me go with you?" asked Agnes. "It is a fête day, or some kind of Church festival, and I would like to go to that lovely church of St. Eustache, where they have the finest organ and sweetest chanting in the world. I know you will like it. It took a hundred years to build the church. It is all just like fairy-land."

As Agnes had been reading the comedies of Molière, the French Shakspeare, she induced Tommy to attend her to the old Théâtre Français, which was under the direction of the great dramatist for many years, and where he was stricken down by death in the middle of a play. It was not open for an exhibition at the hour of the visit, but a courteous Frenchman took them through it, and related to Agnes some pleasing anecdotes of Molière.

The Class took many delightful walks along the clean streets and charming boulevards, visiting churches, public buildings, statues, and paintings. In one of the visits to a church Tommy was much amused  by a priest who, as the people were going out after some superb music, pretended to be praying, but who, amid the noise and confusion was only making contortions of his face. Tommy went through the priest's performance in dumb show when he returned to the hotel for the amusement of Agnes, but was checked by Master Lewis when he attempted a similar imitation in one of the public rooms, lest some one might mistake it for a want of reverence for sacred things.

In one of these walks they were shown a place where a French boy did a noble act at the end of the last war.

An order had been issued to shoot all persons found with arms in their hands in the streets. A captain with his company on duty came upon a French boy with a musket.

"I must order your execution," he said.

"Let me return a watch I have borrowed," said the boy.

"When will you return?"

"At once, upon my word."

The boy went away, and the captain never expected to see him again. But he presently came back, and taking a heroic attitude said, —

"*I am ready, Fire!*"

He was pardoned.

"The young French people," said Master Lewis, "are very patriotic. History abounds with noble acts of French boys. I will relate an incident or two to the point : —

"Joseph Barra lived in the interior of France at the beginning of the French Revolution. He was a generous-hearted boy, who loved truth, his mother, and his country. He was a Republican at heart; a boy of his impulses could have been nothing else.

"Wishing to serve his country in the great struggle for liberty, he entered the Republican army at the age of twelve, as a drummer boy. His whole soul entered into the cause; he was ready to endure any hardship and to make any sacrifice, that the country he loved might be free. He allowed himself no luxuries, but he sent the whole of his pay as a musician to his mother.

"His regiment was ordered to La Vendée to encounter a body of Royalists. One day he found himself cut off from the troops, and surrounded by a party of Royalists. Twenty bayonets were pointed towards his breast. He stood, calm and unflinching, before the glittering steel.

"'Shout,' cried the leader of the Royalists, 'shout, "Long live Louis XVII!" or die!'

"The twenty bayonets were pushed forward within an inch of his body.

"He bent upon his captors a steady eye, kindling with the lofty purpose of his soul. He took off his hat. He gazed for a moment on the blue sky and the green earth. Then, waving his hand aloft, he exclaimed, ' *Vive la République!*'

"The twenty bayonets did their cruel work, and the boy died, a martyr to his convictions of right and of liberty.

"Joseph Agricole Vialla, a boy thirteen years of age, connected himself with a party of French Republican soldiers stationed on the Danube. One day an army of insurgent Royalists were discovered on the opposite side of the river, attempting to cross over on a pontoon. The only safety for the Republican soldiers was to cut the cables that held the bridge to the shore. Whoever should attempt to do this would fall within range of the Royalists' guns, and would be exposed to what seemed to be certain destruction.

"Who would volunteer?

"Every soldier hesitated. The boy Vialla seized an axe, and ran to the bank of the stream. He began to cut the cables amid frequent volleys of shot from the other side, when a ball entered his breast. He fell, but raising himself for a moment, exclaimed, —

"'I die, but I die for my fatherland!'

"In the *Chant du Départ* — an old French revolutionary song, once almost as famous as the *Marseillaise* — the deeds of these boy-heroes are celebrated in the following strain: —

> "'O Barra! Vialla! we envy your glory,
>   Still victors, though breathless ye lie,
> A coward lives not, though with age he is hoary;
>   Who fall for the people ne'er die.
>
> "'Brave boys, we would rival your deed-roll,
>   'Twill guard us 'gainst tyranny then;
> Republicans all swell the bead-roll,
>   While slaves are but infants 'mong men.
>
> "'The Republic awakes in her splendor,
>   She calls us to win, not to fly!
> A Frenchman should live to defend her,
>   For her should he manfully die!'"

Wyllys Wynn seemed much impressed by these incidents of youthful heroism. He sometimes wrote poems, and on his return to the hotel he related the incident of the boy and the watch in these lines, which he read in one of the parlors to Agnes.

HONOR BRIGHT.

The rush of men, the clash of arms,
    The morning stillness broke,
And followed fast the fresh alarms,
    The clouds of battle-smoke.

The Seine still bore a lurid light,
    As down its ripples run,
Where late had shone the fires at night,
    The rosy rifts of sun.

"Shoot every man," the captain cried,
    "That dares our way oppose!"
Like water ran the crimson tide,
    Like clouds the smoke arose.

They forward rushed, the streets they cleared, —
    But ere the work was done,
Before the troop a boy appeared,
    And bore the boy a gun.

"Thou too shalt die," the captain said.
    The boy stopped calmly there,
And sweet and low the music played
    Amid the silenced air.

"Hold!" cried the boy: "a moment wait.
    For, ere I meet my end.
I would return this watch, that late
    I borrowed of my friend."

"Return a watch?" The captain frowned.
    "Your meaning I discern :
Such honest lads are seldom found :
    And when would *you* return?"

"At once!" the hero makes reply;
    "As soon as e'er I can :
I *will* return, and I will die
    As nobly as a man!"

The bugle blew a note of joy,
  "Advance!" the captain cried, —
They marched, and left the happy boy
  The colonnade beside.

We sing Vialla's sweet romance,
  Of Barra's death we read,
But few among the boys of France
  E'er did a nobler deed.

The palace burns, the columns fall,
  The works of art decay,
But deeds like these the good recall
  When empires pass away.

CHAPTER XVI.

BRITTANY.

AVRANCHES. — RIDING ON DILIGENCES. — MONT ST. MICHEL. — CHATEAUBRIAND. — MADAME DE SÉVIGNÉ. — BRITTANY. — BRETON STORIES. — STORY OF THE OLD WOMAN'S COW. — STORY OF THE WONDERFUL SACK. — NANTES. — SCENES OF THE REVOLUTION AT NANTES. — FÉNELON AND LOUIS XV.

THE Class went by rail from Paris to the bright Norman district of Calvados, visiting Caen and Bayeux, whose attractions have been briefly sketched in the letter of George Howe to Master Lewis. The next journey was to Avranches, or the "Village of the Cliff," by the way of Falaise, the residence of Duke Robert, father of William the Conqueror, and to the quaint town of Vire, famous for its cleanly, industrious inhabitants its grand old hills buried in woods, its great wayside trees, and its ancient clock-tower.

The Class met few people on

CLOCK TOWER AT VIRE.

this journey. The cantonniers were evidently busy with their own simple industries. Once or twice the boys saw gentlemen, whom Master Lewis said were curés, at work in cool, green gardens; and often they met the pretty sight of women and girls at work in the fields. The cottages were thatched, and some were moss-grown, and all the canton wore the appearance of simple contentment, virtue, and thrift.

Avranches is a favorite summer resort for English tourists, owing to the beauty of its situation, its health-giving air, and the ease and cheapness with which one may live.

The journey from Caen, along the bowery Norman highways, was made in diligences. The boys seemed to brim over with pleasure at the prospect of a ride in a diligence.

"There is one place where contentment and happiness may surely be found," said Tommy Toby, one day.

"Where?" asked Master Lewis.

"On the top of a diligence."

"Are you sure?"

"Yes, sure."

The next day the Class was overtaken, while travelling in the French coach, by a pouring rain. Tommy, as usual, was on the seat with the driver. He became very impatient, saying, every few minutes, "I wish it would stop raining. I wish—" this, that, and the other thing.

"Tommy," said Master Lewis, from within the coach, "are you sure?"

After a time the sunlight overspread the landscape, making the watery leaves shine like the multitudinous wavelets of the sea.

Tommy's merry voice was heard again, talking bad French.

"Contentment and happiness," said Master Lewis to Frank, "have evidently returned again."

From Avranches the Class visited that wonderful castle, church, and village of the sea, Mont St. Michel.

The journey from the mainland was by a tramway across the Grève, or sands, at low tide. At neap tides the Mount is not surrounded by water at any time, but at spring tides it is washed by the sea twice a day, and sometimes seems like a partly sunken hill in the sea. The fortress is girt about the base with feudal walls and towers colored by the sea; above these rises a little town, the houses being set on broken ledges of rock; above the town stand the fortifications, and a church and its tower crown all. It is one of the most curious places in the world.

Pagan priests here worshipped the god of high places; monks succeeded them; Henry II. held court here, then it became a place to which saints made yearly pilgrimages. The Revolution drove out the monks, and turned it into a prison. In an iron cage called the Cage of St. Michel, a torturous contrivance, state prisoners used to be confined.

The Class next went to St. Malo, by the way of Dol; a breezy journey, with the sea in view.

"St. Malo," said Master Lewis, "was the birthplace of Chateaubriand, who visited our country after the American Revolution, and in 1801 wrote an Indian romance, 'Atala,' a prose Hiawatha, if I may so call it, which charmed all Europe. He published a political work on America, which had great influence in France. He was in early life a sceptic, but the memory of a good mother made him a Christian, and he published a book on religion which arrested the infidel tendencies of the times. Louis XVIII. declared that one of his pamphlets was worth an army of one hundred thousand men. He was one of the most brilliant writers France ever produced. You should read on your return 'Atala' in French. You will find an edition, I think, illustrated by Doré, in which the pictures will compel you to read the story."

"I have read 'Atala,'" said Frank.

"Would you like to visit Chateaubriand's birthplace with me?" asked Master Lewis.

Frank was very desirous to see the place at once, and Master Lewis and he went to the house, now a hotel, immediately on their arrival in the town. From the windows of the house could be seen the tomb of Chateaubriand, which is on a little island in the harbor.

When Master Lewis returned to the hotel he was alone.

"Where is Frank?" asked Tommy.

"He is to spend the night in Chateaubriand's room," said Master Lewis. "Visitors at St. Malo are allowed to sleep there on paying a small sum."

"Is Chateaubriand living yet?" asked Tommy. "I thought you said he came to our country after the Revolution."

"No, he died many years ago. Frank and I have just been looking from the windows of his birthplace at his tomb on one of the little islands."

"But Frank is not going to stay all night in the room of one that is dead! What good will that do?"

"It is the respect that appreciation pays to genius," said Master Lewis.

Ernest Wynn wished to spend the night with Frank, and received Master Lewis's permission.

"Why, Ernest!" said Tommy, "I thought you had more sense. I am glad I am not literary. This is the strangest thing I have met with yet."

Chateaubriand's birthplace is the Hôtel de France. His room is among those offered to visitors, at a little extra cost. Master Lewis had stopped at the hotel during a previous tour.

If Tommy was surprised at the "respect appreciation pays to genius," in the incident of sleeping in Chateaubriand's room, he was more so by a conversation which took place next day, when Master Lewis made his plans for the last zig-zag journeys.

"The last place we will visit," he said, "is Nantes. We will go by rail to Rennes, and by diligences the rest of the way, which will afford you a fine view of Brittany. At Rennes, we will make, if you like, a détour to Vitré."

"What shall we see there?" asked Tommy.

"The residence of Madame de Sévigné."

"Is *she* living?" asked Tommy.

"Oh, no."

"What did she do?"

"She wrote letters to her daughter," said Frank.

"Who was her daughter?"

"The prettiest girl in France."

"Is *she* living?"

"Oh, no," said Frank, impatiently. "Why, did you never hear of the Letters of Madame de Sévigné?"

"I never did. Are her letters there?"

"No."

"What is?"

"The room where she wrote them," said Master Lewis.

"They must be very wonderful letters, I should think," said Tommy, "to make a traveller take all that trouble."

"They are," said Master Lewis. "Lord Macaulay says, ' Among modern works I only know two perfect ones ; they are Pascal's Provincial Letters, and the Letters of Madame de Sévigné.'"

The Class was now in Brittany, a province old and poor, whose very charm is its simplicity and quaintness. Normandy smiles ; Brittany wears a sombre aspect everywhere. Normandy is a bed of flowers; Brittany seems to be a bed of stone. Here and there may be seen a church buried in greenery, but the landscape is one of heath, fern, and broom.

The people are as peculiar as the country. Their costumes are odd, some of them even wear goat-skins. Many of them lead a sea-faring life; it is the Bretons who chiefly man the French navy.

They cling to old legends and superstitions with great fondness;

the wild country abounds with wonder-stories. Nearly all of these stories are striking from their very improbability. They relate to an imaginary period when the Apostles travelled in Brittany, or to men and women who were transformed during some part of their lives into animals, especially into wolves. The story-telling beggars furnish much of the fiction to the unread people.

Those legends which are the chief favorites are undoubtedly very old. The Class listened to several of them at their hotel at St. Malo. Some of them begin in a way that at once arrests attention; as the following story of the

OLD WOMAN'S COW.

When St. Peter and St. John were visiting the poor in Brittany they stopped one day to rest at a farm-house among the trees, where they met a little old woman who kindly brought them a pitcher of cool water.

After the saints had drunk, the old woman told them the story of her hard life. She had seen better days, she said; her husband had once owned a cow, but he had lost it, and he now was only a laborer on the place.

"Let me take the stick in your hand," said St. Peter.

The saint struck the stick on the ground, and up came a fine cow with udders full of milk.

"Holy Virgin!" said the woman. "What made that cow come up from the ground?"

"The grace of God," said St. Peter.

When the saints had gone, the old woman wondered whether, if she were to strike with the stick on the ground, another cow would appear.

She struck the ground as she had seen St. Peter do, when up came an enormous wolf and killed the cow.

The old woman ran after the saints and told her alarming story.

"You should have been content," said St. Peter, "with the cow the Lord gave you. It shall be restored to you."

She turned back, and found the cow at the door, lowing to be milked.

Another story, which greatly pleased Tommy is

THE WONDERFUL SACK.

St. Christopher was a ferry-man. He dwelt in Brittany, at Dol. One day the Lord came to Dol, and wished to cross the river with the twelve Apostles.

St. Christopher, instead of using a ferry-boat, carried the travellers who came to him across the river on his broad shoulders.

When he had thus taken over the Lord and his Apostles, he claimed his reward.

"What will you have?" asked the Lord.

"Ask for Paradise," said St. Peter.

"No," said St. Christopher; "I ask that whatsoever I may desire may at all times be put into my sack."

"You shall have your wish; but never desire money."

One day the Evil One came to St. Christopher, and tempted him to wish for money.

They fell to fighting, and the fight lasted two whole days; but, just as the Evil One seemed about to overcome the saint, the latter said:—

"In the name of the Lord, get into my sack."

In a moment the Evil One was in the sack, and St. Christopher tied the string, and took him to a blacksmith, and requested the use of a hammer.

Then St. Christopher and the smith hammered the Evil One as thin as a penny.

"I own I am *beaten*," said a voice from the sack. "Now let me out."

"That you will never trouble me again."

"I promise."

The ferry-man now began to lead a life of charity. He never thought of himself, but lived wholly for others; and every one loved him, and all that were in distress came to him for comfort.

One day he died, full of years, and, taking with him his wonderful sack, he started for the gates of Paradise.

St. Peter opened the gate. But when he saw that the new-comer was St. Christopher, who had slighted his counsel, he refused to admit him.

The Celestial City, blazing in splendor, stood on the top of a high mountain; the sound of music and the odors of flowers came through the gate as it was opened, and the saint with a heavy heart turned away from all the ravishing beauty, and, hardly knowing what he did, went down the mountain, until he came to the gate of the region where bad souls dwell.

A youth at the gate said to him, —

"Come in."

The gate opened, and the Evil One saw him.

"Shut the gate! shut the gate!" said the Evil One to the youth.

Far, far away the Holy City beamed with ineffable brightness, and up the hill again with a still heavy heart went St. Christopher.

"If I could only get my sack inside the gate, I could wish myself into it; and once inside the gate I could never be turned out."

He came up to the gate again, and called for St. Peter.

The saint opened the gate a little.

"I pray you in charity," said St. Christopher, "let me listen to the music."

The gate was set a little more ajar. Immediately St. Christopher threw into the celestial place the wonderful sack; he wished, and in a

REVOKING THE EDICT OF NANTES.

moment he was in the sack himself,— and he has remained in the region of light, music, flowers, and happiness ever since.

The Class went by rail to Rennes, one of the old capitals of Brittany. It was hardly interesting to them, but a pleasant ride took them to Vitré, where the boys visited the residence of Madame de Sévigné.

Nantes, the ancient residence of the Dukes of Brittany, is situated on the river Loire, about forty miles from the sea. It is one of the largest and most beautiful of the provincial towns of France. In the old castle Henry IV. signed the Edict of Nantes, giving freedom of worship to the Protestants in France.

This famous Edict was published April 13, 1598. The Reformers, or Huguenots, had at this time seven hundred and sixty churches. It was revoked by Louis XIV. in 1685, under the influence of his prelates, who persuaded him thus to seek expiation for his sins. The result of the act was that four hundred thousand Protestants, who were among the most industrious, intelligent, and useful people of France, left the country rather than to give up their religion. They took refuge in Great Britain, Holland, Prussia, Switzerland, and America. From them these countries learned some of the finest French arts.

The Revocation of the Edict of Nantes was one of the many acts of injustice that opened the way for the French Revolution, by destroying public virtue.

Some of the most terrible scenes of the Revolution were enacted at Nantes.

One of the first visits made by the Class at Nantes was to the old warehouse, called the Salorges, built as an entrepot for colonial merchandize, which is associated with the inhuman murders of the Revolution. Here the monster Carrier caused men and women to be tied together and hurled into the Loire, making an exhibition of the cruelty which was known as Republican Marriages. It was in front of the

Salorges that executions by water, called Noyades, were performed. Boats loaded with from twenty to forty victims were towed into the middle of the river, and were sunk by means of trap-doors in their sides, which were opened by cords communicating with the shore. If any of these wretched people attempted to escape by swimming, they were shot. As many as six hundred human beings perished in this way in a single day. The whole number of persons thus destroyed reached many thousands. Women and children were drowned as well as men. The river became so full of bodies that the air was made pestilent.

This was during the dark days of the Reign of Terror, when Marat and Robespierre ruled France. Besides the victims of the Noyades were those who perished in other merciless ways. Five hundred children were shot in a single day, and were buried in trenches that had been prepared for the purpose.

"I do not wonder that Charlotte Corday, who killed Marat, should have been regarded as a heroine," said Frank Gray. "I cannot understand how Frenchmen, who seem to be the most polite, obliging, kind hearted, people in the world, could have been led to do the bloody deeds of the Reign of Terror."

"That is because you have read history too much without thought. In reading history always go back to the causes of things. Read backward as well as forward. All the great palaces in France you have seen were built by the money of an overtaxed people who had no political rights. They were the glittering abodes of immorality. Again and again France was governed by wicked women who became favorites of the king. The Huguenots, who were the sincerely religious people of France, were compelled to leave the nation. Think of it,— four hundred thousand people going away from their native country at the unrestrained edict of one bad man. Do you wonder the people of France desired a Constitution for their protection? The nobler orders of the Catholic Church, the Jansenists and Port Royalists as the

FÉNELON AND THE DUKE OF BURGUNDY.

were called, were also suppressed. The Church became immoral, tyrannical, and almost wholly corrupt, an enemy to the rights of the people. The reaction against such a church, which violated all the precepts of the Gospel, was infidelity.

"During the whole of the reign of Louis XV. the cloud of Revolution was gathering. Louis saw it, but he was so given over to sensuality that it little troubled him. 'These things will last as long as I shall,' he said. '*Après nous le déluge*' (after us the deluge). He was wholly governed, and the nation ruled, by Madame de Pompadour, a corrupt and worthless woman, who made and dismissed ministers of State and cardinals, declared war and dictated terms of peace. She declared that even her lap-dog was weary of the fawnings of nobles. Are you surprised that Frenchmen should rise against such a state of things as this?"

"Was not Louis XV. educated by Fénelon, who wrote *Télémaque*, the French text-book we have been studying?" asked Frank.

"Yes, the most corrupt king of France was educated by the purest and most lovable man of genius that the times produced. The king was a wilful child, but it was thought that Fénelon had quite changed his character by his religious influence. He was subject to what were called 'mad fits.' I might tell you some pleasant stories of this period of his life. One day, when Fénelon had reproved him for some grave fault, he said,—

"'I know what I am, and I know also what you are.'

"Fénelon's prudent conduct quite won back the affection of the child.

"'I will leave the Duke of Burgundy [his title] behind the door when I am with you,' he used to say, 'and I will be only little Louis.'

"Fénelon turned the boy's mind to piety, and for a time influenced him by it. 'All his mad fits and spites,' he said of his pupil, 'yielded to the name of God.'

"But Fénelon, like all good and pure men of the time, was con-

THE CATHEDRAL AT NANTES

LOUIS XV.

vain. He was once ill, and on his recovery all Paris was filled with rejoicing. An immense crowd gathered around the palace on the eve of St. Louis's Day in honor of the convalescence. As the boy-king stood on the balcony of the palace on the occasion, Marshal Villeroy said to him, —

"' Look at all this company of people : all are yours ; they all belong to you ; you are their master.'

"Think of a boy's being told that the people of Paris belonged to him!

"I can wonder at the Reign of Terror, but I cannot be surprised at the Revolution when I view the history of France for the century that preceded it. It is rather a matter of surprise that an enlightened people should have submitted to tyranny so long."

Nantes is the Paris of the Loire. Its streets, boulevards, public squares, the forest of masts in the river, and the trees that line its banks, all seem a copy of the bright and gay French capital. Its old cathedral is a queer-looking building, with towers scarcely higher than its roof; but it contains a most beautiful tomb which was erected in memory of Francis II. last Duke of Bretagne. It is adorned with figures of angels, the twelve Apostles, St. Louis, and Charlemagne.

One of the most interesting excursions made by the Class from Nantes was to the ruin of the old castle of

BLUE-BEARD.

There existed, many centuries ago, a ferocious, cruel old lord, whose treatment of his wives and ogre-like tyranny to all around him, gave origin to the thrilling story of Blue-beard ; indeed, the story was so nearly true that this old lord was actually called " Blue-beard " by his neighbors, so blue-black was his long and stubby beard.

He lived in the old days when barons were fierce and despotic, and shut their wives and daughters up in dark dungeons or high castle casements, and thought little more of ordering a score of peasants off to instant execution than of eating their breakfasts.

He was a rich old fellow, and had several castles scattered about the country, whither princes and dukes used to go **and** visit him, and share in his hunting-parties **in** the wildwoods.

His castles were situated **in the** province of **Brittany,** and his real name was one which is still **to** be found in these secluded regions, — the Sieur Duval. The lapse of time has caused all his fine castles wholly to disappear, with one exception, and it is that which **I** am about to describe to you.

Sieur Duval had his favorite residence **on the banks** of a lovely little river, about two miles from Nantes. Here he was near town, and might ride in on one of his **high-tempered** chargers **whenever** he listed, to join the revels of the dukes, **or go** wife-hunting.

It was at this castle **that his** cruelties **to** his **unhappy** spouses are supposed to have occurred; **and** it was from Nantes that **the** brother of his **last** wife **is** said **to have** ridden **in hot** haste **to** rescue his wretched sister and make **an end** of the **odious old** tyrant.

Taking a row-boat by the high, old **bridge which,** just on the outskirts of Nantes, spans **the river** Erdre, you **find** yourself at first on a broad sheet of water, **with** quaint, whitewashed **stone-houses** and huts their roofs covered **with red** brick tiles, and occasionally more handsome mansions with lawns **and** gardens extending to the riverbank. Here you may perhaps **observe a** row **of** curious flat-boats with roofs, but open on all sides, lining **both** banks **of the stream.** In these are **a** number of hard-featured, dark-skinned women of all ages, washing clothes. They lean over the boat-sides, and **scrub** the shirts and handkerchiefs in the water, then withdraw them, lay them smoothly on some flat boards, like a table, and taking a flat hammer pound upon them.

Presently you get past these, if you row vigorously, and come to pretty bends in the river, and find yourself beyond the thickly-settled part, amidst pleasant rural fields, with some wealthy merchant's mansion raising its towers above the green trees.

After a while you approach a bright little village, all of whose houses form a single street just along the banks of the river. Here you disembark and pass along the village street, across a rickety bridge which spans a little inlet from the stream, and so out into the country, and through paths in the woods thickly grown with brush and wildflowers.

Presently, soon after you have got out of sight of the village, you ascend a gentle hill, and suddenly come upon an old, old house, with its wooden ribs appearing, crossing each other, through the stone walls, and a roof that looks as if about to fall in upon the people who inhabit it.

Just beyond this, deeply imbedded in shrubs, brush, thickly-grown ivies and other vines, and moss, is all that is left of Blue-beard's castle.

The walls are still there, dividing the apartments. You can imagine the rooms and the tower which arose above the tall trees that here cluster on the river bank. And you may fancy, as you stand among the beautiful ruins, that you are on the very spot where the room used to be which Blue-beard forbade his last wife to enter.

Here is the portal, now crumbled and almost covered with moss and ivy, where the old tyrant came in and out; there the wall where the last of his poor victims sat, looking out and straining her eyes to see her brother coming; beyond, the spot where Blue-beard was struck down, and received his deserts. It seems too beautiful a place for so remorseless an ogre; and as one looks out upon the lovely scenes where the tearful spouses mourned their lot, one cannot help thinking how happy they might have been in such a charming retreat, had they enjoyed it with loving husbands and happy homes.

CHAPTER XVII.

HOMEWARD.

On the Cliffs at Havre.—Stories of French Authors.—Again on the Sea.

"ONLY three days more remain to us in France," said Master Lewis, after spending two days in Nantes. "We will now return to Paris by rail, stopping a few hours in Orleans, and from Paris will go directly to Havre, whence we will take the steamer for home."

"It seems to me," said Wyllys Wynn, "that, after what we have seen, I shall like no reading so well as history."

"It has been my aim," said Master Lewis, "to take you to those places where the principal great events of the histories of England and France have occurred. I stopped at Carlisle to give you a lesson in the early history of Britain,—the periods of the Druids and the Romans. I took you to Glastonbury to give you a view of the history of the early English Church. I went with you to Aix-la-Chapelle that you might receive an impression of the dominion of Charlemagne. Normandy is the common ground of old English and French history. I was glad to select it for you as the direct object of our visit, although it has formed a small part of our journey. I, like Tommy, have had a secret which I have kept for the Club; it has been to interest you in the places and events which would lead you, on your return, to become more careful readers of the best books. I hope the journey will leave an historic outline in your minds that future reading will fill. Character is as much determined by the books one reads as by the company one keeps. Show me a boy's selection of books, and I will tell you what he is and what he is likely to become."

"Master Lewis," said Wyllys, "says he has aimed to take us to such historic places as would give us, at the end of the journey, a connected picture of English and of French history. Let us try to associate the places we have seen with historic events. As I think of our Scottish and English journey, I connect,—

"Carlisle with the Druids and Romans.

"Glastonbury with Early Christianity and the Boy Kings.

"Normandy with William the Conqueror and his sons.

"Nottingham with Robin Hood and the Norman and Plantagenet Kings.

"Boscobel with King Charles.

"Edinburgh with Mary, the Edwards, and the Douglases.

"Kenilworth with Elizabeth.

"Oxford with Canute and Alfred.

"London with the Tudors, the Commonwealth, the Georges, and Victoria."

"In our journey on the continent," said Frank, " I associate,—

"Brussels with Waterloo and Napoleon.

"Aix-la-Chapelle with Charlemagne.

"Ghent and Bruges with the Dukes of Flanders and Burgundy.

"Calais with Mary Tudor and Edward III. of England.

"Rouen with Charles VII. and Joan of Arc.

"Paris with Charles IX., the Bourbons, and Napoleon.

"Nantes with the Huguenots and the Revolution."

"We have also had views of the homes and haunts of great authors," said Ernest. "I have made a scrap-book of leaves and flowers from the homes and graves of men of letters, and it includes souvenirs of nearly all the most eminent names in English literature."

Havre is really a port of Paris, and is one of the most thriving maritime towns of France. Like most port towns it is more business-

MOLIÈRE

the vermilion of the sky. The boys were sober at the thought that this was their last day in Europe, and that they were now to return to the set tasks of the school-room.

"These cliffs," said Master Lewis, "were the favorite haunts of the author of 'Paul and Virginia.' He was a mere theorist, a day-dreamer; and here he loved to gaze on the bright sea, and plan expe-

THE READING OF "PAUL AND VIRGINIA."

ditions of republican colonists to such lands as he paints in his novels. His expeditions ended in the air. But he himself went to Mauritius, where he lived three years. On his return to Paris, while the brightness of tropical scenery still haunted him, he wrote 'Paul and Virginia.'"

"When Corneille, the great Corneille, as the popular dramatist came to be called, read his masterpiece, *Polyeucte*, to a party of fashionable literary people in Paris, it was coolly received on account of the fine Christian sentiments it contained. The criticism was that the religion of the stage should be that, not of God, but of the gods. Even a bishop present took this view.

"Bernardin de St. Pierre was as sharply criticised when he first read in public his beautiful romance of 'Paul and Virginia.' It was at a party given by Madame Necker. 'At first,' says a writer, 'every one listened in silence; then the company began to whisper, then to yawn. Monsieur de Buffon ordered his carriage, and slipped out of the nearest door. The ladies who listened were ridiculed when tears at last gathered in their eyes.'

"*Polyeucte* still lives in French literature, and the wits who condemned it are forgotten; 'Paul and Virginia' charmed France; fifty imitations of it were published in a single year, and it was rapidly translated into all European tongues. It remains a classic, but the critics in Madame Necker's parlors are recollected only for their mistake."

"We must read the works of these French authors on our return," said Wyllys, "or at least the best selections from them. I shall wish to read 'Pascal's Provincial Letters' and the Letters of Madame de Sévigné, after what you have said of them."

"You should also read some of the best selections from the works of Boileau, Molière, and Racine. I have only time to allude to them briefly here.

"These authors were friends. They all lived in the time of the

Grand Monarch, as Louis XIV. was called. La Fontaine, some of whose fables you have read, belongs to the same period, which is the greatest in French literature.

"Louis XIV. appreciated nearly all the great writers of the time; he seems to have felt that great authors, like great palaces, would add lustre to his reign."

"I think that we might better change our society on our return into a reading-club," said Tommy Toby.

"It seems to me your proposal is a very good one," said Master Lewis. "We may be able to travel again. If we should visit Germany or the Latin lands together another year, a reading-club would be an excellent preparation for the journey."

"Very much better than a Secret Society," said Frank. "Suppose you give the Class the secret you devised for our first meetings, Tommy."

"Oh," said Tommy, soberly, "that, like most of my other plans, was just *nothing, after all.*"

Away from busy Havre the next morning, under the French and American flags, moved a little ocean world; and on the decks, looking back to the fading shores of old Normandy, and cherishing delightful memories of their zigzag journeys in historic lands, were the teacher and the lads whose winding ways we have followed.

CELEBRATED WAR STORIES.

THE BOYS OF '61.

Or Four Years of Fighting. A record of personal observation with the Army and Navy from the battle of Bull Run to the fall of Richmond. By CHARLES CARLETON COFFIN, author of "The Boys of '76," "Our New Way 'Round the World," "The Story of Liberty," "Winning His Way," "Old Times in the Colonies," etc. With numerous illustrations.

1 vol., 8vo, chromo-lithographed board covers and linings $1.75
1 vol., 8vo, cloth, gilt 2.50

THE SAILOR BOYS OF '61.

By Prof. J. RUSSELL SOLEY, author of "The Boys of 1812," etc. This volume contains an accurate and vivid account of the naval engagements of the great Civil War, and the deeds of its heroes. Elaborately and beautifully illustrated from original drawings.

1 vol., 8vo, chromo-lithographed board covers, ... $1.75
1 vol., 8vo, cloth gilt, . . 2.50

THE BOYS OF 1812.

By Prof. J. RUSSELL SOLEY, author of "Blockaders and Cruisers," "The Sailor Boys of '61," etc., etc. This "most successful war book for the young, issued last year," is now made boards with an illustrated cover designed by Barnes.

1 vol., 8vo, chromo-lithographed board covers . . . $1.75
1 vol., 8vo, cloth gilt, . . 2.50

"Prof. SOLEY's books should be read by every American boy, who cares for the honor of his country." — *Boston Beacon.*

"He must be a dull boy who can read such records of heroism without a quickening of the pulses." — *San Francisco Chronicle.*

"We are in no danger of cultivating too much patriotism, and such a book as this is an excellent educator along an excellent line of thought." — *Chicago Daily Inter-Ocean.*

The Sixth Mass. Regiment passing through Baltimore.

MY DAYS AND NIGHTS ON THE BATTLEFIELD.

By CHARLES CARLETON COFFIN. With eighteen full-page plates. Small quarto. Bound in illuminated board covers. $1.25

FOLLOWING THE FLAG.

By CHARLES CARLETON COFFIN. With eighteen full-page plates. Small quarto. Bound in illuminated board covers, ... $1.25

WINNING HIS WAY.

By CHARLES CARLETON COFFIN. With twenty-one full-page plates. Small quarto. Bound in illuminated board covers, ... $1.25

THE CARLETON SERIES OF JUVENILES,

CONSISTING OF

WINNING HIS WAY.   FOLLOWING THE FLAG.
MY DAYS AND NIGHTS ON THE BATTLEFIELD.

3 vols., 16mo, cloth, in a box, ... $3.75
Any volume sold separately, ... 1.25

ESTES & LAURIAT, Publishers, BOSTON, MASS.

THE FOUR GREAT ANNUALS.

CHATTERBOX FOR 1891.

This name, a household word in every home in the land, has become endeared in the hearts of many generations, and the readers of the early volumes are now men and women, who know that no works will delight their children more, or instruct them to a greater extent, than these dear old annual volumes, whose sales have long since mounted above the million mark.

This authorized reprint from duplicates of the original English plates, contains a large amount of copyright American matter, which cannot be reprinted by any other firm.

The Genuine Chatterbox contains a great variety of original stories, sketches and poems for the young, and every illustration which appears in it is expressly designed for this work, by the most eminent English artists. It has over 200 full-page original illustrations.

This year, to add to the enormous sales, no expense or trouble have been spared in securing a paper that would do entire justice to this royal juvenile, and make the illustrations appear to their best advantage, and it possible, bring the book nearer the zenith of juvenile perfection.

1 vol., quarto, illuminated board covers,	$1.25
1 vol., quarto, cloth, black and gold stamps,	1.75
1 vol., quarto, cloth, extra, chromo, gilt side and edges,	2.25

LITTLE ONES ANNUAL.

Illustrated Stories and Poems for the Little Ones Edited by WILLIAM T. ADAMS (Oliver Optic). This beautiful volume consists of original stories and poems by the very best writers of juvenile literature, carefully selected and edited. It is embellished with 370 entirely original illustrations, drawn expressly for the work by the most celebrated book illustrators in America, and engraved on wood in the highest style, under the superintendence of George T. Andrew.

1 vol., quarto, illuminated board covers,	$1.75
1 vol., quarto, cloth and gilt,	2.25

"Little Ones Annual is by all odds the best thing of the season for children from five to ten years old."— *Boston Journal.*

THE NURSERY—T.

For 26 years the Nursery has been welcomed in thousands of families as the favorite picture book for our little folks, and the best of it is it improves in quality every year. It is now enlarged in size and crowded with charming stories and original artistic illustrations. Edited by OLIVER OPTIC

1 vol., royal octavo, illuminated covers,	$1.25

OLIVER OPTIC'S ANNUAL, 1891.

A volume edited by OLIVER OPTIC appeals at once to the heart of every boy and girl, with all of whom his name is a synonym for everything bright and entertaining in juvenile literature.

This is the leading book of its kind of the year, with original illustrations.

1 vol., quarto, illuminated board covers and frontispiece,	$1.50

ESTES & LAURIAT, Publishers, BOSTON, MASS

ENTERTAINING JUVENILES.

SCHOOLBOYS OF ROOKESBURY;
Or, The Boys of the Fourth Form. An entertaining story of the mishaps and adventures of several boys during a term at an English school. Edited by LAWRENCE H. FRANCIS. Fully illustrated with original drawings.
1 vol., small quarto, illuminated board cover $1.25

QUEEN HILDEGARDE ;
By LAURA E. RICHARDS, author of " Four Feet, Two Feet, and No Feet " A new edition of this popular girl's book, — a second " Little Women, " — containing nineteen illustrations from new and original drawings.
1 vol., small quarto, illuminated board covers $1.50
" *We should like to see the sensible, heroine loving girl in her early teens who would not like this book. Not to like it would simply argue a screw loose somewhere.* " — BOSTON POST.

THE DAYS OF CHIVALRY;
Or, Page, Squire and Knight. A highly interesting and instructive, historical romance of the Middle Ages. Edited by W. H. Davenport Adams, author of " Success in Life, " " The Land of the Incas, " etc. Thoroughly illustrated with 113 drawings.
1 vol., small quarto, illuminated board covers $1.50

THE RED MOUNTAIN OF ALASKA.
By WILLIS BOYD ALLEN. An exciting narrative of a trip through this most interesting but little known country, with accurate description of the same. Full of adventures, vividly portrayed by choice, original illustrations, by F. T. Merrill and others.
1 vol., 8vo, cloth, gilt, ... $2.50
" *It throws 'Robinson Crusoe', the 'Swiss Family Robinson', and all those fascinating thantasies, hopelessly into the shade, and will hold many a boy spellbound, through many an evening, of many a winter.* " — CHICAGO TRIBUNE.

HUNTING IN THE JUNGLE
With Gun and Guide. From Les Animaux Sauvages, by WARREN F. KELLOGG. An exciting and amusing series of adventures in search of large game — gorillas, elephants, tigers and lions — fully illustrated with over a hundred original drawings by celebrated artists, engraved on wood by the best modern book illustrators.
1 vol., 8vo, chromo-lithographed board covers $1.75
1 vol., 8vo, cloth, gilt, ... 2.50

OUR NEW WAY 'ROUND THE WORLD.
By CHARLES CARLETON COFFIN, author of " The Story of Liberty, " " The Boys of '61, " " Following the Flag, " " The Boys of '76, " " Winning His Way, " " My Days and Nights on the Battlefield, " etc., etc. A new REVISED edition of this standard book of travel, which is interesting and useful to young and old; with a large number of additional illustrations.
1 vol., 8vo, chromo-lithographed board covers, ... $1.75
1 vol., 8vo, cloth, gilt, ... 2.50

TRAVELS IN MEXICO.
By F. A. OBER. A brilliant record of a remarkable journey from Yucatan to the Rio Grande Historic ruins, tropic wilds, silver hills are described with eloquence. No country possesses so rich a field for the historian, antiquarian, fortune-hunter, and traveller.
1 vol., 8vo, chromo-lithographed board covers $1.75
1 vol., 8vo, cloth, gilt, ... 2.50

DICKENS'S CHILD'S HISTORY OF ENGLAND.
Holiday edition, with 100 fine illustrations, by De Neuville, Emile Bayard, F. Lix, and others.
1 vol., 8vo, chromo-lithographed board covers $1.75
1 vol., 8vo, cloth, gilt, ... 2.50

THE YOUNG MOOSE HUNTERS.
By C. A. STEPHENS, author of the " Knockabout Club in the Tropics, " etc., etc. With numerous full-page original illustrations made expressly for this edition. An exciting account of a hunting trip through the Maine woods.
1 vol., small quarto, illuminated board covers $1.50

SIX GIRLS.
By FANNY BELLE IRVING. A charming story of every-day home life, pure in sentiment and healthy in tone. A beautiful book for girls Fully illustrated from original designs.
1 vol., small quarto, illuminated board covers and linings. $1.50

HANS CHRISTIAN ANDERSEN'S FAIRY TALES.
The standard authorized edition. A new translation from the original Danish edition, complete and unabridged, fully illustrated with engravings made from the original drawings, with an appropriate cover designed by L. S. IPSEN.
1 vol., quarto, cloth. $2.25

FEATHERS, FURS AND FINS;
Or STORIES OF ANIMAL LIFE FOR CHILDREN. A collection of the most fascinating stories about birds, fishes and animals, both wild and domestic, with illustrations drawn by the best artists, and engraved in the finest possible style by Andrew.
1 vol., quarto, chromo-lithographed board covers, ... $1.75
1 vol., quarto, cloth and gilt, ... 2.50

ESTES & LAURIAT, Publishers, BOSTON, MASS.

THE FAMOUS ZIGZAG SERIES.

The Most Entertaining and Instructive, the Most Successful and Universally Popular Series of Books for the Young Ever Issued in America.

Over Three Hundred Thousand Volumes of the Series have already been sold in this Country alone.

It is Vacation

Zigzag Journeys in Australia;

Or, a Visit to the Ocean World. Describing the wonderful resources and natural advantages of the fifth continent, giving an insight into the social relations of the people and containing stories of gold discoveries and of the animals peculiar to this fascinating country.

1 vol., small quarto, illuminated board covers and hinges, ... $1.75
1 vol., small quarto, cloth, bevelled and gilt, . - 2.25

Uniform in style and price with the above, the other volumes of the series can be had as follows:

Zigzag Journeys in the Great North-West;

Or, a Trip to the American Switzerland. Giving an account of the marvelous growth of our Western Empire, with legendary tales of the early explorers. Full of interesting, instructive and entertaining stories of the New Northwest, the country of the future.

Zigzag Journeys in the British Isles.

With excursions among the lakes of Ireland and the hills of Scotland. Replete with legend and romance. Over 150 illustrations.

Zigzag Journeys in the Antipodes.

It's some time tae 'the reader to Siam, and with delightful illustration and anecdote, tells him of the interesting animal life and of the country. Ninety-six illustrations.

Zigzag Journeys in India;

Or, the Antipodes of the Far East. A collection of Zenana Tales. With nearly 100 fine original illustrations.

Zigzag Journeys in the Sunny South.

In which the Zigzag Club visits the Southern States and the Isthmus of Panama. With romantic stories of early discoveries and discoverers of the American continent. Seventy-two illustrations.

Zigzag Journeys in the Levant.

An account of a tour of the Zigzag Club through Egypt and the Holy land, including a trip up the Nile, and visit to the ruins of Thebes, Memphis, etc. 114 illustrations.

Zigzag Journeys in Acadia & New France.

In which the Zigzag Club visits Nova Scotia and Acadia — "the Land of Evangeline," — New Brunswick, Canada, the St. Lawrence, Montreal, Quebec, etc., with romantic stories and traditions connected with the early history of the country. 102 illustrations.

Zigzag Journeys in Northern Lands.

From the Rhine to the Arctic Circle. Zigzag Club in Holland, Belgium, Germany, Denmark, Norway, and Sweden, with picturesque views, entertaining stories, etc. 119 illustrations.

Zigzag Journeys in the Occident.

A trip of the Zigzag Club from Boston to the Golden Gate; including visits to the wheat-fields of Dakota, the wonders of the Yellowstone and Yosemite. 148 illustrations.

Zigzag Journeys in the Orient.

A journey of the Zigzag Club from Vienna to the Golden Horn, the Euxine, Moscow, and St. Petersburg; containing a description of the Great Fair at Nijni-Novgorod, etc. 142 illustrations.

Zigzag Journeys in Classic Lands;

Or, Tommy Toby's Trip to Parnassus. An account of a tour of the Zigzag Club in France, Italy, Greece, Spain, and Portugal. 124 illustrations.

Zigzag Journeys in Europe;

Or, Vacation Rambles in Historic Lands. In which the Zigzag Club travels through England, Scotland, Belgium, and France; with interesting stories and legends. 126 illustrations.

ESTES & LAURIAT, Publishers, BOSTON, MASS.

THE FAMOUS VASSAR GIRL SERIES.

☞ "Mrs. Champney's fame as the authoress of the delightful series of travels by the 'Three Vassar Girls,' has extended throughout the English-speaking world."

Three Vassar Girls in the Tyrol.
An entertaining description of the travels of our Vassar friends through this well-known country, giving an interesting account of the Passion Play at Ober Ammergau. Illustrated by "Champ" and others.
1 vol., small quarto, illuminated board covers and linings, ... $1.50
1 vol., small quarto, cloth, bevelled and gilt, . 2.00

Uniform in style and price with the above, the other volumes of the series can be had as follows:

Three Vassar Girls in Switzerland.
By ELIZABETH W. CHAMPNEY. An exceedingly interesting story interwoven with bits of Swiss life, historic incidents, and accounts of happenings at Geneva, Lucerne, and the Great St. Bernard. Illustrated by "Champ" and others.

Three Vassar Girls in Russia and Turkey.
During the exciting scenes and events of the late Turko-Russian war, with many adventures, both serious and comic. Profusely illustrated from original designs, by "Champ" and others.

Three Vassar Girls in France.
A story of the siege of Paris. A thrilling account of adventures when Germany and France were engaged in their terrible struggle. Ninety-seven illustrations by "Champ," Detaille, and De Neuville.

Three Vassar Girls at Home.
Travels through some of our own States and Territories, with many interesting adventures. Ninety-seven illustrations by "Champ."

Three Vassar Girls on the Rhine.
Full of amusing incidents of the voyage and historic stories of the castles and towns along the route. 128 illustrations by "Champ" and others.

Three Vassar Girls in Italy.
Travels through the vineyards of Italy, visiting all the large cities, and passing some time in Rome, in the Vatican, the Catacombs, etc. 107 illustrations.

Three Vassar Girls in South America.
A trip through the heart of South America, up the Amazon, across the Andes, and along the Pacific coast to Panama. 112 illustrations.

Three Vassar Girls in England.
Sunny memories of a holiday excursion of three college girls in the mother country, with visits to historic scenes and notable places. Ninety-eight illustrations.

Three Vassar Girls Abroad.
The vacation rambles of three college girls on a European trip for amusement and instruction, with their haps and mishaps. Ninety-two illustrations.

THE NEW SERIES.

Great Grandmother's Girls in New Mexico.
By ELIZABETH W. CHAMPNEY. This is the second volume of this delightful series describing incidents in the life of a quaint little maiden who lived in the time of the Spanish adventurers. Illustrated by "Champ."
1 vol., 8vo, chromo-lithographed board covers . $1.75
1 vol., 8vo, cloth, gilt 2.50

Great Grandmother's Girls in France.
By ELIZABETH W. CHAMPNEY. A charming volume for girls, consisting of romantic stories of the heroines in the early colonial days—their privations and courage.
1 vol., 8vo, chromo-lithographed board covers . $1.75
1 vol., 8vo, cloth, gilt, ... 2.50

"A beautiful volume and one that cannot fail to arouse intense interest."—*Toledo Blade*.

"An excellent present for a boy or girl."—*Boston Transcript*.

ESTES & LAURIAT, Publishers, BOSTON, MASS.

THE FAMOUS "KNOCKABOUT CLUB" SERIES.

"Delightful and wholesome books of stirring out door adventure for healthy American boys, books whose steadily increasing popularity is but a well earned recognition of intrinsic merit."

THE KNOCKABOUT CLUB ON THE SPANISH MAIN.

By FRED A. OBER. In which the Knockabout Club visits Caracas, La Guayra, Lake Maracaibo, etc. Containing stories of the exploits of the pirates of the Spanish Main. Fully illustrated.

1 vol., small quarto, illuminated board covers and linings, . $1.50
1 vol., small quarto, cloth, bevelled and gilt, . . . $2.00

Uniform in style and price with the above, the other volumes of the series can be had as follows:

THE KNOCKABOUT CLUB IN NORTH AFRICA.
By FRED A. OBER. An account of a trip along the coast of the Dark Continent, caravan journeys, and a visit to a pirate city, with stories of lion hunting and life among the Moors. Fully illustrated.

THE KNOCKABOUT CLUB IN SPAIN.
By FRED A. OBER. A panorama of Seville, the Guadalquivir, the Palaces of the Moors, the Alhambra, Madrid, Bull-fights, etc. Full of original illustrations, many full-page.

THE KNOCKABOUT CLUB IN THE ANTILLES.
By FRED A. OBER. A visit to the delightful islands that extend in a graceful line from Florida to South America, accompanied by a "Special Artist." 78 illustrations.

THE KNOCKABOUT CLUB IN THE EVERGLADES.
By FRED A. OBER. A visit to Florida for the purpose of exploring Lake Okechobee, on which trip the boys encounter various obstacles and adventures with alligators, etc. 55 illustrations.

THE KNOCKABOUT CLUB IN THE TROPICS.
By C. A. STEPHENS. From the ice-fields of the North to the plains of New Mexico, thence through the "Land of the Aztecs," and the wonderful ruins of Central America, to the "Queen of the Antilles." 103 illustrations.

THE KNOCKABOUT CLUB ALONGSHORE.
By C. A. STEPHENS. A journey alongshore from Boston to Greenland, with descriptions of seal-fishing, Arctic Scenery, and stories of the ancient Northmen. 137 illustrations.

THE KNOCKABOUT CLUB IN THE WOODS.
By C. A. STEPHENS. A boy's book of anecdotes and adventures in the wilds of Maine and Canada. An account of a vacation spent in healthy amusement, fascinating adventure, and instructive entertainment. 117 illustrations.

ESTES & LAURIAT, Publishers, BOSTON, Mass.

YOUNG FOLKS' HISTORIES

YOUNG FOLKS' HISTORY OF THE NETHERLANDS.
A concise history of Holland and Belgium, from the earliest times, in which the author goes over the ground covered by Motley in his standard histories of these most interesting countries, and brings the narrative down to the present time. By ALEXANDER YOUNG. 150 illustrations.

YOUNG FOLKS' HISTORY OF AMERICA.
From the earliest times to the present. A new edition. With a chapter and additional illustrations on the Life and Death of President Garfield. Edited by H. BUTTERWORTH, author of "Zigzag Journeys." With 157 Illustrations. Over 10,000 copies sold in one year.

YOUNG FOLKS' HISTORY OF MEXICO.
Comprising the principle events from the sixth century to the present time By FRED. A. OBER, author of "Camps in the Caribbees." With 100 illustrations.
The intimate relations of our country with Mexico, which the railroads and mines are developing, make this volume one of the most important in the entire series.

YOUNG FOLKS' HISTORY OF RUSSIA.
By NATHAN HASKELL DOLE. With 110 illustrations.

THE GREAT CITIES OF THE WORLD.

YOUNG FOLKS' HISTORY OF LONDON.
With graphic stories of its historic landmarks. By W. H. RIDEING. With 100 illustrations.

YOUNG FOLKS' HISTORY OF BOSTON.
By H. BUTTERWORTH, author of "Zigzag Journeys," etc. With 140 illustrations.

CHARLOTTE M. YONGE.   YOUNG FOLKS' HISTORIES.

YOUNG FOLKS' BIBLE HISTORY. With 132 illustrations.
YOUNG FOLKS' HISTORY OF ENGLAND. With 60 illustrations by De Neuville, E. Bayard and others.
YOUNG FOLKS' HISTORY OF FRANCE. With 84 illustrations by A. De Neuville, E. Bayard and others
YOUNG FOLKS' HISTORY OF ROME. With 114 illustrations.
YOUNG FOLKS' HISTORY OF GREECE. With 51 illustrations.
YOUNG FOLKS' HISTORY OF GERMANY. With 82 illustrations.

YOUNG FOLKS' EPOCHS OF HISTORY.

YOUNG FOLKS' HISTORY OF THE CIVIL WAR.
A concise and impartial account of the late war, for young people, from the best authorities both North and South. By MRS. C. EMMA CHENEY. Illustrated with 100 engravings, maps and plans.

YOUNG FOLKS' HISTORY OF THE REFORMATION.
IN GERMANY, FRANCE, ENGLAND AND OTHER COUNTRIES By FRED H. ALLEN. A graphic account of the men and the movements by which the great religious revolution which resulted in the establishment of Protestantism was carried on, from the early centuries of Christianity to the end of the Reformation. Fully illustrated.

YOUNG FOLKS' HISTORY OF THE QUEENS OF SCOTLAND.
These valuable books are condensed from Strickland's Queens of Scotland by ROSALIE KAUFMAN, and are at once reliable and entertaining to both old and young folks. Fully illustrated. 2 vols., 16mo, cloth. . . $3.00.

YOUNG FOLKS' HISTORY OF THE QUEENS OF ENGLAND.
From the Norman Conquest. Founded on Strickland's Queens of England. Abridged, adapted and continued to the present time. By ROSALIE KAUFMAN. With nearly 300 Illustrations. 3 vols., 16mo, cloth . $4.50.

LIBRARY OF ENTERTAINING HISTORY.
Edited by Arthur Gilman, M. A.

INDIA. By FANNIE ROPER FEUDGE. With 100 illustrations, .	$1.50
EGYPT. By Mrs. CLARA ERSKINE CLEMENT. With 108 illustrations,	1.50
SPAIN. By Prof. JAMES HERBERT HARRISON. With 111 illustrations, . .	1.50
SWITZERLAND. By Miss HARRIET D. S. MACKENZIE. With 100 illustrations,	1.50
HISTORY OF AMERICAN PEOPLE. With 175 illustrations.	1.50

All the above volumes are published as 16mos, in cloth, at $1.50.

ESTES & LAURIAT, PUBLISHERS,
BOSTON, MASS.

HOUSEHOLD NECESSITIES.

SOCIAL CUSTOMS.

New edition, REDUCED IN PRICE. Complete Manual of American Etiquette. By FLORENCE HOWE HALL, daughter of Mrs. Julia Ward Howe. Handsomely printed, and neatly bound in extra cloth, gilt top, uncut. Small 8vo. • • • • • • $1.75

DO YOU ALWAYS KNOW JUST WHAT TO DO? Do you know how to encourage Mrs. D. Lightful, accept and return her courtesies, as they deserve; and politely but firmly avoid and defeat Mrs. Bore in her inroads on your privacy and more agreeable engagements? If you do not, let us recommend for EVERY SOCIAL QUESTION the above entertaining and instructive book, or its new baby relative, "THE CORRECT THING," mentioned below, for with these two books, one can make no mistake in life, as every possible question may be answered from their combined wisdom. They are *comprehensive, practical, reliable and authoritative*.

THE CORRECT THING.

By FLORENCE HOWE HALL, author of "Social Customs." 18mo. Very neatly bound in extra cloth, gilt top, • • • • • • • • $0.75
Same. Bound in full flexible morocco, gilt edges (in a box). • • • • $1.25

This new manual is neatly printed in a size not too large to be slipped into the pocket, and is arranged so that one page reminds the reader that "IT IS THE CORRECT THING" to do this, while *per contra* the opposite page tells him that "IT IS NOT THE CORRECT THING" to do that. Its conciseness recommends it to many who would not take the time to master any more comprehensive manual.

"It is, indeed, a treasure of good counsel, and, like most advice, it has the merit of not being expensive."—*Montreal Gazette.*

PARLOA'S KITCHEN COMPANION.

A GUIDE FOR ALL WHO WOULD BE GOOD HOUSEKEEPERS.

Handsomely printed, and very fully illustrated. Large 8vo. (nearly 1000 pages). Neatly bound in extra cloth or in waterproof binding. • • • • • • $2.50

☞ "It is thoroughly practical; it is perfectly reliable; it is marvellously comprehensive; it is copiously illustrated. It is, in short, overflowing with good qualities, and is just the book that all housekeepers need to make them.

Miss Parloa's new book has proved a remarkable success, and it could hardly have been otherwise. Exhaustive in its treatment of a subject of the highest importance to all, the result of years of conscientious study and labor upon the part of one who has been called "the apostle of the *renaissance* in domestic service," it could not be otherwise than welcome to every intelligent housekeeper in the land.

"This is the most comprehensive volume that Miss Parloa has ever prepared, and, as a trusty companion and guide for all who are travelling on the road to good housekeeping, it must soon become a necessity. . . . . No amount of commendation seems to do justice to it."—*Good Housekeeper.*

PARLOA'S NEW COOK BOOK AND MARKETING GUIDE.

12mo. Cloth. • • • • • • • $1.50

This is one of the most popular Cook Books ever printed, containing 1724 receipts and items of instruction. The directions are clear and concise, and the chapters on marketing and kitchen furnishing very useful.

ESTES & LAURIAT, PUBLISHERS.
BOSTON, MASS.

www.ingramcontent.com/pod-product-compliance
Lightning Source LLC
Chambersburg PA
CBHW030739230426
43667CB00007B/776